NONVERBAL
COMMUNICATION

COMMUNICATION SCIENCE
AND TECHNOLOGY

*Designed for Communication Leaders in the Media, Libraries
and Information Specialization*

PATRICK R. PENLAND, *Editor*

NONVERBAL COMMUNICATION

FOR MEDIA, LIBRARY AND INFORMATION SPECIALISTS

Ellen Steele McCardle

EDITED BY PATRICK R. PENLAND

Illustrations by Paul B. Edwards

MARCEL DEKKER, INC. New York 1974

MARCEL DEKKER, INC.

270 Madison Avenue, New York, New York 10016

LIBRARY OF CONGRESS CATALOG CARD NUMBER: 73-90766

ISBN: 0-8247-6126-X

Current printing (last digit):
10 9 8 7 6 5 4 3 2 1

PRINTED IN THE UNITED STATES OF AMERICA

COMMUNICATION SCIENCE AND TECHNOLOGY

An Introduction to the Series

Since midcentury there has been an exponential increase in the volume of recorded knowledge and a revolution in the control and transfer of information by means of electronic technology. These changes have not only brought the resource specializations of media, library, and information science into a closer working relationship, but have been the impetus for the creation of a new profession, that of resource communicator. Resource sharing and computer networking have made it difficult for these three specializations to hang onto outmoded autonomies. Creative professionals have been released by technology to explore their role as advocates and agents of change in the affairs of human beings. This commonality of concern for people, as distinct from the production, control, and transfer of materials, is slowly being articulated by leaders in the three specializations.

The common profession of communicator, whose objective is to develop communication services based on a network of all-encompassing resource infrastructures, has emerged from the specializations of media, library, and information science. In practice, of course, some variations may still exist in the services provided. With this series these variations need no longer receive greater attention than the needs of the whole human being seeking help for his own behavioral self-control and self-design. As a result, the client need no longer be shunted around from media center to library and adult-education agency or to information center regardless of the fact that it is the surprise value of knowledge within a behavioral context which he needs and not necessarily the documents and resources guarded by each type of resource agency.

The general purpose of publications in the Communication Science and Technology series is to integrate professional and historical developments, as so many other texts in the field do not. These publications feature a service-oriented and conceptually-interlocking system of communication principles and communication services based within the traditions and practice of media, libraries, and information science. Publications in the series provide the basis for a bold new approach for the resource communicator, one which emphasizes communication over agency standards, deals directly with the problems of living rather than with documentation, and meets controversy when and where it arises in the neighborhood without traveling to the media, library, or information center.

The disciplines that create new knowledge will be interested in this approach to the development of communications. The profession of re-source communicator holds considerable promise as a significant social method for more rapidly closing the gap between research findings and their application to the affairs of the common man. In addition, the series will be of singular importance to any profession which employs the re-sources of recorded knowledge to solve human problems or develops guidelines for planned social change, such as is done in education, com-munications, and politics. A case in point is adult education, the prin-ciples and methods of which have long served as a source of inspiration and guidance to librarians. These professions can view the emergence of resource communicators not as an encroachment upon their affairs but as an opportunity for enhanced partnership in serving public needs.

These publications can be employed as guides for practice, in-ser-vice training, and the continuing education of resource-center staff. The theoretical foundations of behavioral psychology, group-systems analysis, and community sociodrama will be of particular significance to the busy supervisor called upon to provide a rationale for communication services in media, libraries, and information centers. Within this framework the methods and techniques are developed for creating, chan-neling, and applying information surprise to the concerns and interests of the patron whether as an individual, a small group, or the neighbor-hood and community enterprise.

These publications will help the profession to create the conditions within which communicative activity can occur. Through communication, it will enhance its image as a socially accountable profession which can handle socially unstable subsystems. More specifically, the reader, be he general or professional, will find answers to questions such as the following.

What social purposes, function, and even, procedures do the resource professions share with each other and with other professions in society?

For what social change among which publics are the
resource professions responsible? Within what contexts can the change process be carried out by resource communicators?

What means can be employed to accomplish planned
social change? What factors can be exploited in order
to motivate citizens to participate and to communicate?

How can the infrastructure of resources be deployed in
order to support a communications profession? How can
the gap between indexed message space and the nonverbal
and audio-visual message space of the people be closed?

The volumes in the series may be used as textbooks, supplementary
readings, or as background reading for the informed citizen, especially
the wide range of persons who use media, libraries, and information
centers as well as those who serve as trustees or board members of institutions which maintain resource centers. The volumes in the series
cover concepts and describe methods that would be useful in particular
for

Audiovisual and media specialists in a wide range of
centers serving patrons with various socioeconomic,
cultural, and educational levels

Librarians in all types of agencies and who provide
services to patrons of varying age levels, education,
and socioeconomic status

Information specialists, including systems analysts and
designers, at various levels of service

The broad range of adult education facilities administered by
a variety of institutions and agencies as well as educators
at all levels and, in particular, media and library and information science faculties

Sociologists, political scientists and politicians, urban-
ologists and urban information systems specialists

Community planners (urban planners), public administrators, community leaders (lay and professional),
communication specialists (all levels)

Professional staff and lay volunteers of the numerous
information hot lines and neighborhood information
centers

The models presented and the methods discussed are fundamental
to human affective and cognitive development as it is achieved through
communicative processes. The professional concerned about his own
self-development may wish to peruse these publications for insight into
what is known about human intellectual growth and development. As a
result he may be able to remain in control of his own growth, independent
of outside influences. On the other hand, in those instances when he
finds it useful to seek help from other communicators, the professional
role will become more meaningful and productive for him.

Since the meaning of communication is not self-evident, the resource
professions need a definition and explication of a communicative profession and the relation of applications to the contexts of dyad, group,
and community. With a formulated behavior theory integrated with the
principles of media, library and information science it should be possible
to increase the scope of communication within the mainstream of social-
science research. While many of the examples are taken from "adult"
education as well as the resource specializations, other communicators
will find the approach particularly appropriate to a wide range of human
development professions.

Communications specialists will look to this approach in order to
conceive of their professional difficulties in communication terms and
realize that encounter negotiation and information surprise are the fundamental components of relevance. In general, the many exercises and
simulations are designed to be readily understood by and acceptable to
staff members, while at the same time avoiding the limitation of single
examples without a conceptual framework. The professional methods
of human communication are presented within the psychology of the behavioral cycle. Human-relations training, group dynamics, and decision
making are immersed in small-group sociology. Community psychology
and coordination support the professional methods of persuasion, mass
communication, advocacy, and community development.

PREFACE

When Dr. Patrick Penland invited me to contribute to the series "Communication Science and Technology" I accepted with enthusiasm. Specialists in the media, library and information sciences are to be commended for their concern with this vital aspect of interpersonal relation and its role in their professional endeavors. Skills, expertise, and knowledge are vacuous without appropriate means of conveyance and the evolution of a body of theory in human communication for these specialists is a most commendable project.

Generally, behavior may be considered as movement through space and time; how and why that movement is effected, in what direction, at what pace, under what motivation, become warp and woof in the tapestry of human behavior. Communication, in all its guises, is an essential element in the process. We are inclined to consider communication primarily in its spoken or written modality yet this is only one level of expression; linguistic variance, kinesic behaviors, visceral changes all combine in the totality of the communication process. For this reason it is impossible to consider kinesics, or nonverbal communication, as a singular entity; this explains the sometimes divergent subject areas which follow.

When we can begin to perceive these interrelationships as a part of the natural order in the universe about us, and, in particular, the order which prevails in smaller segments of that universe, we may better envision our place within it. The insight thus gained is priceless. The quality of our individual fulfillment in space and time gains new meaning and we are enabled to participate more fully in the human community. Agassiz advised "Study nature, not books." We may learn the rudiments of behavior and communication theory from written accounts; real comprehension comes during the pursuit of our various endeavors.

ACKNOWLEDGMENTS

I wish to express appreciation to Dr. William S. Condon and Dr. Felix F. Leeb for the training in nonverbal communication I received from them at Western Psychiatric Institute and Clinic, Pittsburgh. Under their tutelage the world of silent language came to reveal a scope and complexity at times awesome, always fascinating. Dr. Condon and Dr. Leeb had earlier participated in a linguistic-kinesic research program established by Dr. Henry W. Brosin. As Chairman of the Department of Psychiatry, School of Medicine, University of Pittsburgh, Dr. Brosin provided an atmosphere in which research could be pursued, ideas discussed, and concepts developed. His dedication to research and education, the noblest of services, produced others highly skilled in their interest areas. For those who, in turn, have been trained by them the rewards have been great. The excellent quality maintained by the Pittsburgh Psychoanalytic Institute is evident in the works of Doctors Coleman and Leeb cited. Members and faculty of that institute have contributed without measure their time and talents to teaching others.

Paul Edwards claims he is not an illustrator. However he is to be commended for the drawings he has provided. Mr. Edwards is head of the Art Department, Washington and Jefferson College, Washington, Pennsylvania.

CONTENTS

To him who in the love of Nature holds

Communion with her visible forms,

     she speaks

A various language

          William Cullen Bryant

            - Thanatopsis

NONVERBAL
COMMUNICATION

ONE

SYSTEMS IN HUMAN COMMUNICATION

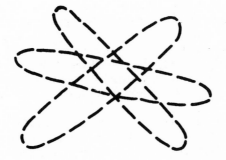

INTRODUCTION

It is impossible for living humans not to communicate. From the
first ex utero wail to the final moment of being each of us communicates in an infinite variety of modes. The small child laughs delight-
edly as he chases a balloon, conveying pleasure and well-being; the
autistic child with quiet lips communicates response to his environment with darting eyes or slight muscular movement. As the pretty
coed hurries to class her shining eyes and ready smile bespeak self-
assurance; the catatonic patient signals anxiety so intense that it can
only be contained by rigid immobility. A spectator at a sporting
event cheers his team; riding home on a bus he exchanges glances
and superficial conversation with fellow passengers; at dinner he relates more intimately with his family; later, at his workbench, he
sands a piece of driftwood to be hung as a wall ornament. In each
situation he is communicating, to others, from and about himself.
And he is receiving communications from the environment, so that a
constant interplay - dynamic, everchanging - persists.

Humans have been communicating for thousands of years, and
they have long been aware of the subtleties in nonverbal communication. The Greek theater is sometimes characterized by its tragi-
comedy masks. Sir Francis Bacon (1) described gestures as "natural hieroglyphic writing in the air." Estienne, a sixteenth century
French linguist, noted the gesture assimilation or "italianization
effect" upon the French by Italian courtiers (11). The word "physio-
gnomic," referring to the practice of judging character and mental
abilities by scrutiny of the facial and bodily features, is derived
from a combination of the Greek physis, nature, and gnomen, one
who knows, acknowledging a natural observation method of analysis.

SCHOOLS OF COMMUNICATION THEORY

The twentieth century, however, has spawned a surge of interest
in the study, research, and theory of human communication. It has
been described in political terms, by mathematical formulas, with
existential mystique, as symbolic interaction. Theories have evolved
ranging from communication as a monologic unit to those concerning

the mass media, sometimes disturbingly termed "mass persuasion."
These theoretical approaches tend to group into a few major categories.

Mechanistic Theories

The mechanistic orientation views communication as a thoroughly
describable "entity," by the application of mathematical or cyberne-
tic formulations. Thus it is explained in such terms as series of
transmittals and receptors via a channel replete with feedback loops,
entropy, and measurement calibration. While these theories may be
useful in charting flow of information, they do not allow for relevant
variables in the total communicational process as, for example,
affect or the emotional state, perception, or the context in which the
interchange occurs. They are not particularly well suited to the
study of nonverbal behaviors.

Psychological Theories

The psychological group of theories includes the familiar stimu-
lus/response (S/R) model, dealing with the conscious, cognitive
level of communication. This model carries an implication of control through the manipulation of environmental stimuli. Game theory
is another in this group, based on a principle of reward-punishment
in communicational interaction. The experimentalists have designed
studies in which behavior, and thus communication, are influenced
toward some particular performance set, accomplished through the
manipulation of certain variables.

In contrast to the mechanistic approach, the psychological group
of theories does recognize and include the environment as a significant factor, albeit one which may be altered by the experimenter, so
that some degree of artificiality occurs. Psycholinguistic theory
combines the S/R paradigm with some aspects of the mechanistic
school: there is a message which is decoded and a response which is
encoded. These psychological approaches are generally action-
reaction models and may well have evolved from the structure of our
English language, the subject-verb-object sequence. Their weakness for use in nonverbal studies lies in their isolation of variables,
with the result that the total communicational situation is not considered. The result is a reductionist, "meiotic" approach.

Systems Theories

In attempts to find answers, to explain the nature of the universe and things within it, man has often resorted to dualistic thought - Apollonian-Dionysian, Yin-Yang, Heaven-Hell, psyche-soma. Efforts to integrate opposing forces have been made: Yin and Yang, for example, are explained in Chinese religious philosophy as the primigenial elements from which the universe evolved, and both are present in any individual or entity. Western man, particularly since the Enlightenment, has tended toward a closed-system logic. The early Judeo-Christian dichotomy found reinforcement in Descartes' res cognitans and res extensa, the dualism of mind and matter. These Cartesian categories were more than antithetical concepts; they exemplified the isolation of an element from the whole. The Newtonian method further preserved the discretizing and separation of elements. This reductionist approach has led to many advances; it has surely produced great eras of technology and discovery. But in digitally pinpointing singulars we have sometimes failed to recognize pluralities and their interrelationships.

The open systems approach to communication acknowledges an integrated pluralism, an organizing of parts into their natural entirety. The isolation of elements may still be utilized, not as the ultimate goal, but to establish their relationship, or function, or significance, to the totality. Moreover, "open" denotes an exchange between the system and the environment, recognizing the dynamic nature of their interrelationship. The systems method offers a blending of portions of the mechanistic and psychologic orientations, but it also includes the social setting -- the context. Within this framework the S/R, or encoder-decoder, is recognized, but as a portion of the gestalt, the total operational field. This is a more sociologic approach, for it includes the dyadic or group process which is occurring in combination with other simultaneous levels of communication. Hence it relates to the concept of system, with two or more individuals forming a unit or organization which differs from the sum of the individual behaviors, due to the incorporation of the process itself. This systems approach bespeaks a recognition of the complexity of human interaction, its many facets and levels, and the dynamic quality of human communication.

Historical Perspective

To establish a framework for the understanding of nonverbal communication we may review the evolvement of general systems theory. The early twentieth century, notably the post-World War I era, became a time for new beginnings in several fields. Psychology, dissatisfied with the narrow confines of behaviorism and the atomistic approach, began to seek broader horizons for describing human behavior. The gestalt approach had been touched upon earlier by William James and John Dewey. In 1890 James drew an analogy remarkably similar to later developments.

In a sense a soap bubble has parts; it is a sum of juxtaposed spherical triangles. But these triangles are not separate realities. Touch the bubble and the triangles are no more. Dismiss the thought and out go its parts. You can no more make a new thought out of ideas that have once served you than you can make a new bubble out of old triangles. Each bubble, each thought, is a fresh organic entity, sui generis. (16)

Dewey, in his reflex-arc paper (1896), urged the study of the whole situation rather than a contrived stimulus-response analysis. He favored a view of behavior as a total coordination which adapts the organism to the situation (10). The reflex-arc is described as an organic entity which loses its original reality and meaning when subjected to analysis, an observation similar to that stated in Bohr's Law of Complementarity: a rigorous space-time description and a rigorous causal sequence for individual processes cannot be simultaneously realized (9).

The gestalt school flourished with the work of Max Wertheimer (1880-1943), a German psychologist. He, too, rebelled at the constricted methods of behaviorism, choosing to theorize the structure of experience as an organized whole, influenced in large part by the manner in which it is perceived. In 1922 he stated:

The given is itself in varying degrees structured (Gestaltet), it consists of more or less definitely structured wholes and whole-processes with their whole-properties and laws,

characteristic whole-tendencies and whole-determinations
of parts. Pieces almost always appear as parts in whole
processes. (20)

Hartmann (15), in describing the role of independent systems,
stresses that "the laws of science are the laws of systems, i.e.,
structure of finite extent -- a generalization applicable to both physics and psychology." Gestalt psychology has frequently employed
the term 'field,' a nebulous and overworked term borrowed from the
fields of force defined in physics. The concept of organization is
similarly stressed, and prediction focuses on behavior being dependent upon the situation, as a whole, at any particular time, or as an
experience of the whole organism. Lewinian field theory expanded
these concepts, resulting in a systematized theory of life-space -
the totality of factors at a particular point in time. It relates patterns of organization to total behavior, the isolation of single conditions not considered to provide an overall view. To summarize, then,
behavior is dynamic and so must be analyzed within the total field in
which it occurs. Only then may specific elements and relationships
be studied separately.

Other disciplines were pursuing similar lines of inquiry. In 1921
Ruth Benedict began a comparative anthropological study of diverse
traits within each of several cultures. These traits were found to
group into larger social orders, each culture having selected certain
characteristics for elaboration. The selected traits account for a
culture's uniqueness. Benedict also recognized the interdependency
of the individual and his society -- "The whole determines its parts,
not only their relation but their very nature" (2). Others in anthropology followed this trend; that particular discipline has consistently
supported the systems concept of pattern and order.

Structural linguistics describes a sophisticated organization of
language established by Bloomfield and Sapir and continued by Pike,
Wells, McQuown, Harris, Smith, Trager, and others. Harris de-
tails "the logic of distributional relations" and considers it to constitute the basic method of structural linguistics (14). Speech is thus
comprised of discrete parts ordered into larger units which, in turn,
evolve into a "structured discourse." He notes "correlations between the system as a whole, or features of it, on the one hand, and
data from outside the descriptive order on the other" (14, page 374).

Kurt Goldstein, a psychiatrist, provided an astute conceptualization of part/whole relationships as applied to human behavior. He described the individual as an organism whose behavior is an entity involving the total personality. Only abstractly can behavior be segmented into parts -- bodily processes, conscious or unconscious phenomena, states of feeling, attitudes. Rather, the "phenomenon of behavior" becomes understandable when viewed as a totality governed by the "trend to actualize itself," i.e., its nature and its capacities (12). So any stimulation to the organism, either of an environmental or an internal nature, creates a state of disorder rectified through a process of "equalization," contributing to the constancy of the organism. The individual personality corresponds to this constancy and also determines by which means equalization will be effected. Goldstein favors yielding the notion of separate drives to a view of the total organism's "figure-ground organization of capacities" (13).

Molecules group into cells, thence into tissues, organs, organ systems. These systems integrate in a functional process within the organism, the individual. He in turn belongs to a family, the primary system providing a foundation for identifications, values, perceptions, and a host of other enculturalizing factors. From this milieu he enters school and becomes a member of that system; he joins a social group and takes on a role unique to that group. So throughout the life cycle his rank, role, participation in a variety of systems shifts and alters as he also does. Varied relationships exist between these interacting systems and they, too, change over time. For these are open systems with ongoing exchange of material and energy. Closed systems subsist in the domain of physics, and perhaps even they will be found related if a unified field theory combining electromagnetic and gravitational equations as proposed by Einstein can be developed.

This open systems approach offers a sound method for the integration of theory and knowledge concerning organism, man, and social group. It may be applied to a range of subjects and situations. Von Bertalanffy (3) considers it to be applicable "to all psychobiological and psycho-cultural phenomena." Systems theory facilitates understanding of situations concerning any human group -- the family, a work setting, a library or hospital staff, and larger organizations as, for example, a political party or the cause and effect relationships between major political factions. It is necessary to view human communication in this manner if we are to grasp the totality of the process.

Study of Nonverbal Communication

The natural history method of research in nonverbal communication began at the Center for Advanced Study in the Behavioral Sciences, Stanford University, Palo Alto, California, in 1956. In her efforts to teach psychiatric residents the interplay between deductive and intuitive processes, Freda Fromm- Reichmann discussed the problem with other professionals. A study group formed, leading to a disciplined "think tank" research effort, including psychiatrists Fromm-Reichmann and Henry Brosin, anthropologists Gregory Bateson and Ray Birdwhistell, linguists Charles Hockett and Norman McQuown. Their concentrated analysis of a filmed nontherapeutic interview represents a minute study of every aspect of the interaction, as well as the interrelation, of all levels, revealing facets of complexity in the communicational process never before realized (18). Smith and Trager at the University of Buffalo were also involved in these early, intensive studies of linguistic and kinesic behavior. This, then, was the beginning of a scientific inquiry into the detailed, micro study of communicational behaviors.

Pattern and Levels of Organization

As their research progressed and sound films were utilized for micro analysis, Albert Scheflen, working in close alliance with Ray Birdwhistell in Philadelphia, added a rich new dimension to the work through a refinement of the systems approach. Here communication was described as culture, broadening the system to include the concept of organization within the parts. So rules, traditions, regulation of the communicational process above and beyond the messages, motivations, and perceptions of the participants are included. This method permits the inclusion of ethnic, class, and sexual variables, and their particular constellations of behavior. These constellations, or clusters, of behavior appear to occur in successive levels of patterning, their purpose being to modify, amend, define, or facilitate human relationships and communication. While the social structures comprising these relationships are not visible, the communicational activities which signify and maintain them are discernible both audially and visually. Structural linguistics and kinesics are thus combined and included as parts of the total system. The organization of fairly constant recurring units is seen as the structure of communication, while the change and maintenance of equilibrium evolve into the concept of system.

We will consider nonverbal behaviors in this manner -- as part of the total, dynamic, open system of communication, a system comprised of variables which may be isolated for study but which, in toto, form a gestalt. Interestingly, gestalt may be translated as "pattern," and there is, indeed, pattern, order, regularity in the communicational process -- a process of "multiple behavioral patterns existing on different time levels," as Birdwhistell notes (4). These patterns permit "cross-referencing" of communicative phenomena as well as analysis of the exact structural meaning.

Pattern denotes an arrangement of forms, a grouping or disposition of parts, and thus leads to the concept of levels of patterning in human communication. It is important to stress here the term 'level' rather than 'hierarchy,' for the latter carries an implication of domination, each unit subordinate to the next higher in rank, a governing-governed relationship. In our consideration of communication it seems more appropriate to speak of levels, of multi-level communication, of levels of organization, a set of ordered levels, etc. For 'level' signifies "an assembly of things of a definite kind, e.g., a collection of systems characterized by definite properties and laws, and such that it belongs to a line of biological descent" (6). So each level possesses certain characteristics, unique properties, which interact with other levels in a coherent integration of parts.

Rhythmicity

The nonverbal repertoire is but one level in the total communicational stream, integrating with all other levels -- linguistic, affective, etc. Each of these levels comprises a system bearing unique attributes, pattern, structure. And while the various levels may differ in content, they show isomorphism in their structural aspects. There is organization in the relationship among the levels, so that they combine in a configuration of interlocking systems. These various modalities are operating simultaneously, although perhaps at different rates and rhythms. Condon and Brosin (7) have termed this phenomenon "the whiles" -- while the vocal system emits a sound the shoulder may rise, the fingers move almost imperceptibly, the eyes blink, the foot taps. All of these behaviors are highly organized into a communicational stream of behavior. "The body moves in 'configuration-of-change' which are isomorphic with the articulated segments of speech as they are articulated" (8).

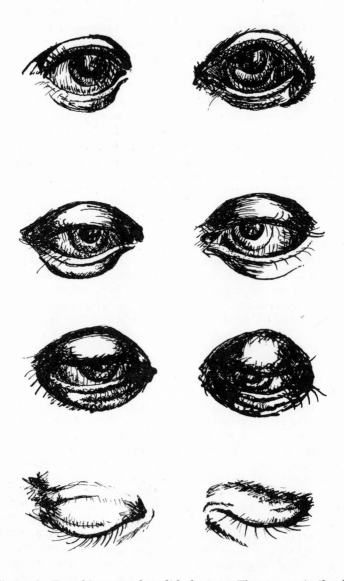

Figure 1. Four kinemes of eyelid closure. There are similar kinemes for the nose, mouth, and facial areas, as well as for other body parts — the hand, shoulders, trunk, leg and foot, etc.

Individual Synchrony. Kinesic behaviors are not random, unrelated movements but are, themselves, highly organized systems. There are levels in the nonverbal system, too. Kines, basic elements of body motion, group into allokines or kinemes (see Figure 1); these are similar to the phones and phonemes of linguistics. Kinemes organize into kinemorphs, which, at the next higher level, group into kinemorphic classes. Hence, a complex kinemorphic construction may possess many properties of the syntactic sentence [see Table 1]. There is a rhythmicity to body movement, partially determined by cultural influence, coupled with idiosyncratic features. So one individual may move with sinuous grace, another with awkward motion, another in constricted cadence. For each of them kines, kinemes, kinemorphs have organized to create a complex construction which we perceive as body movement and rhythm, an individual system of self-synchrony.

TABLE 1

LINGUISTIC UNITS	KINESIC UNITS
Phone	Kine
Phoneme	Kineme (allokine)
Morpheme	Kinemorph
Syntactic sentence	Kinemorphic construction

Another systematization, described by Scheflen (19), also relates kinesic behavioral levels. The point refers to typical individual kinesic of the head, particularly the eye region. Most Americans have three to five point configurations which they use repetitively. These points are the distinguishing facial configurations of an individual. Others quickly learn to recognize, and even anticipate, the point configurations of family members, friends, and work partners with no conscious effort. Points serve a signal function essential to human bonding mechanisms and to the regulation of communication. The position is the next higher level, consisting of several points in sequence. A position is usually held from one half-minute to five or six minutes. Most people communicate out of two-four postural

stances, their individualized positions. The presentation is one's
total postural and expressive "gestalt," ranging in time from several
minutes to several hours, terminals marked by a change in location
or context. Scheflen emphasizes that a sociocultural point is a
"communicational structural event," culturally established and readily recognized among members, while a personality point is an individualized behavior (see Table 2).

Interactional Synchrony. But these individual levels are not all of
nonverbal behavior. For people interact, signifying an inherent re-
ciprocity of linguistic and kinesic systems. As contrasted with self-
synchrony, this is interactional synchrony, and it appears to be a
universal phenomenon, as noted in micro study of film segments from
various cultures and ethnic groups. We humans seem guided by
some inner pilot to pick up another's rhythm, as he also tunes in to
ours, so that recognition and regulation occur rather quickly. It is a
"communicational fit," and it enhances the ongoing communicational
process even though it may not be consciously realized. Even

TABLE 2

IDIOSYNCRATIC LEVELS	IDIOKINESIC LEVELS
Words, phrases	The Point: facial configura-tions, particularly the eye region; typical head posture
Sentence	The Position: gestures, arm positions
Larger units of speech: individual speech behavior	The Presentation: seated and standing postures, postural stances

periods of silence may attest to a state of rapport, noted in shared
postures or movements. The tune "Shall we dance?" comes to mind
as one becomes alert to these rhythmic synchronous behaviors ei-

ther as a participant or as an observer of others in interaction.
Here again, open systems are influencing and being influenced by
other open systems, abiding by all the biosocial maxims of general
systems theory.

Unfortunately, well-modulated interactional synchrony does not
always occur; a communication mis-fit is then the consequence.
Class, racial, and ethnic differences in these subtle movements and
rhythms may contribute to a dys-synchrony, or cacophony. It is to
this point that we may particularly address ourselves as we delve
further into our investigation of nonverbal behaviors. For there are
ecological systems, too, and we bear the stamp of our eco-niche or
biotope, with all its innuendoes of past influence on present behavior.
Konrad Lorenz (17) has noted the difference in "polite listening"
between residents of Vienna and Konisberg. He was at first puzzled
by the military stance of residents in the latter city -- head held
high, eyes directed straight at his face. He came to realize this was
a somewhat exaggerated subcultural variation of the general listening
stance.

Birdwhistell (5) has documented differing "health sets," connot-
ing kinesic expression of illness, in two Kentucky communities only
15 miles apart. Residents of Dry Ridge utilize the "stiff upper lip"
configuration with retraction of the scalp, tightening of the forehead
skin, and a hyper-erect posture. Green Valley inhabitants discuss
their malaise more readily, and their kinesic illness behavior is
noted in medial compression of the brows, sag of the eyelids and
cheeks, upper torso and shoulders out of tonus. Modicum differen-
tials, yes -- but significant factors in the degree of affinity or
estrangement which may be sensed during an interactional sequence.

SUMMARY

We will be considering nonverbal behavior as an open system
within the larger communicational complex, one part of the whole,
with each having pattern, order, organization. Human communication bears a striking analogy to musical counterpoint form: several
voices, or parts, occurring simultaneously. There is conjunct
movement with varied intervals, repetitions of themes and subthemes,
a cadence to mark completion of a sequence. An understanding of
the part played by kinesic behaviors in this contrapuntal performance
can assist in our appreciation of the dynamic interplay of the total
communicational anlage.

REFERENCES

1. Francis Bacon. Of the Advancement and Proficiency of Learning (ed. of 1640). Oxford: Yound and Forrest, Book VI, pp. 258-259.

2. Ruth F. Benedict. Patterns of Culture (rev. ed.). Boston: Houghton Mifflin, 1959, p. 52.

3. Ludwig von Bertalanffy. Organismic Psychology and Systems Theory. Barre, Massachusetts: Clark Univ. Press and Barre Publishers, 1968.

4. Ray L. Birdwhistell. Kinesics and Context. Philadelphia: Univ. of Pennsylvania Press, 1970, p. 88.

5. Ray L. Birdwhistell, "Kinesics in the context of motor habits." Paper presented before the American Anthropological Association, December 28, 1957. Also in Kinesics and Context. Philadelphia: Univ. of Pennsylvania Press, 1970.

6. Mario Bunge, "Hierarchical Structures," Proceedings of Symposium held Nov. 18-19, 1968 at Douglas Advanced Research Laboratories. Huntington, California: (L. L. Whyte, A. G. Wilson, and D. Wilson, eds.). New York: Elsevier, 1969, p. 19.

7. William S. Condon and Henry W. Brosin, "Micro Linguistic-Kinesic Events in Schizophrenic Behavior." In Schizophrenia: Current Concepts and Research (D. V. Siva Sankar, ed.). Hicksville, New York: PJD Publications, 1969, pp. 812-837.

8. William S. Condon and W. D. Ogston, "A segmentation of behavior." J. Psych. Research, 5, 221-235, 1967.

9. A. D'Abro. The Rise of the New Physics. New York: Dover Publications, 1951, p. 951.

10. John Dewey, "The Reflex-arc concept in psychology," Psych. Rev., 3, 357-370, 1896.

11. Henri Estienne. Deux Dialogues du Nouveau Langage Francois Italianize et autrement desguize, principalement entre les courtisans de ce temps (2 vol.). Paris: Liseux, 1883.

12. Kurt Goldstein. Human Motives in the Light of Psychopathology. Cambridge: Harvard Univ. Press, 1940, p. 194.

13. Kurt Goldstein. The Organism: A Holistic Approach to Biology. New York: The American Book Co., 1939, 249 ff.

14. Z. S. Harris. Structural Linguistics. Chicago: Univ. Chicago Press (Phoenix Books), 1951.

15. G. W. Hartmann. Gestalt Psychology. New York: Ronald Co., 1935, p. 42.

16. William James. The Principles of Psychology. New York: Holt & Co., 1890, Vol. 1, p. 279, footnote.

17. Konrad Lorenz. On Aggression. New York: Harcourt Brace & World, 1966, p. 81.

18. Norman A. McQuown (ed.). The Natural History of an Interview (with contributions by Gregory Bateson, Ray L. Birdwhistell, Henry W. Brosin, Charles F. Hockett, and Norman A. McQuown), in "Microfilm Collection of Manuscripts on Cultural Anthropology," Univ. of Chicago, 1971.

19. Albert E. Scheflen, "The significance of posture in communicational systems." Psychiatry, 27, 316-331, 1964.

20. Max Wertheimer (1922), as translated in A Sourcebook of Gestalt Psychology (A. D. Ellis, ed.). New York: Harcourt Brace & World, 1938, p. 14.

TWO

THE BIOLOGY OF BEING

GENERAL STATEMENT

Biology is a science particularly suited to a study of communication at all levels. Man is a being whose form and function, growth and development, demonstrate him to be essentially a biologic entity sharing attributes of physical life with countless other living forms. But man is unique due to significant additions -- his mental attributes compose a suprastructure interrelated with his physical composition, facilitating a profound and diverse range of abilities. By virtue of these particular properties he is the only product of biological evolution capable of influencing, and even controlling, his own destiny. Genetic endowment is enhanced by social creations, transmitted generationally, with alterations and sophistications occurring over time. Human values, ethics, a sense of morality, are certainly human qualities which transcend the biological. But this array of human creations evolves from, and builds on, the basic biologic structure.

This background for our approach to communicational behavior conveys a sense of enthusiasm, even excitement, as consideration of the vast range of potential for communication unfolds. Our seemingly infinite capacity to adjust to multiple exigencies, and even grow in the process, bespeaks our potential for further progress in improving the quality of life. Biological constructs guide us toward a better understanding of many natural phenomena which may, in turn, be utilized in the service of man.

Ethology is a relatively recent addition to the biological sciences; Lorenz has described it succinctly as "the biology of behavior" (6, page xi). It is grounded in the work of Charles Darwin (1872) and Alfred Russel Wallace (1858), an English naturalist. Both men noted that the emotions of higher animals, including man, contained operative elements formed into a unitary and patterned organization. It should be noted, however, that Darwin and Wallace related emotion to the expression of feeling states, and were primarily concerned with their origin (6, page 366). Charles Otis Whitman and Oscar Heinroth established a theoretical base for the budding science of ethology, and significant contributions by von Frisch, von Uexkull, Craig, Huxley, Lorenz, Tinbergen, Hinde, and others, followed.

Early ethological efforts were directed toward intensive study of animal behaviors. In recent years, particularly since 1950, ethological theory has been extended to include the highest species, Man. His unique psychic organization necessitates its inclusion as an added dimension to be assimilated into existing ethological theory. The Freudian psychology of the spontaneity of instincts, of the interplay between psychic processes and experience, and the role of ego as mediator between id and superego, serves to elucidate this significant factor.

RELEVANT PRINCIPLES FROM BIOLOGY

The intensive study and research of nonverbal behaviors is also a recent area of specialization. Ethological studies have contributed significantly to nonverbal communication research and theory. Some general principles of biology may be considered as they relate to nonverbal behaviors.

Structure

Structure pertains to the manner in which parts are assembled to form a unit. Ethology is concerned with the phylogenetically determined roots of a behavioral unit and how it has changed, under selection pressure, to what it is today. The descriptive term homologous is often used in comparative statements regarding behavior patterns, referring to their similarity in structure due to a common origin. Certain adult motor patterns may be traced to infantile movements and thus are homologous in motor form. A popular query as to structure is "How come?"

Function

Function deals with the purpose a behavior or a group of behaviors serve. Kinesic behaviors sometimes serve to regulate the communicational process or assist in establishing mutuality between or among participants. They may reinforce the verbal message or they may contradict it. They may even reflect an unconscious co-existent association seemingly unrelated to the verbal material. Analogous signifies a similarity in function between parts which are dissimilar in origin; it also is frequently used to signify a partial resemblance between two behavioral units. The succinct question here is "What for?"

Adaptation

Adaptation connotes change of some kind from an original form
to subsequent variants. These changes enhanced survival in the
early days of man; they continue to facilitate his accomodation to the
physical, social, and cultural environment. There is necessarily
a continuous interplay between environment and adaptation. It is important to note that no organism changes in order to fit the environment and thus to survive; rather the organism survives and adapts
because of change. The human hand did not evolve to its highly
specialized form so that it could perform kinesic gestures, but it
can do so because of its specialization in differential action, oppos-
able thumb, degree of wrist supination and extension, etc.

Man possesses a remarkable capacity for adaptiveness in his
behavioral range. One soon acquires some of the linguistic mannerisms, accents, stress variations, and modifiers of an area setting.
Some have noted they "take on" a gesture, manner, affectation of a
friend, teacher, business associate with whom they have repeated
contact. These are individual adaptations and they occur throughout
one's lifetime -- ontogenetic adjustments. Our species similarly
adapts itself to changing conditions over generations; these are
phylogenetic adaptations. They occur more slowly, over a longer
period of time.

Selection

Selection is concerned with the survival value of a structure or
function. In nonverbal behavior, selection has determined which
motor patterns, postures, gestures will best serve as expressive
behaviors. These have often become compressed into ritualized
units, dropping many of the original components so that only rudiments of the earlier pattern remain. Huxley (7) describes this
ritualization as "the adaptive formalization or canalization of
emotionally motivated behavior, under the teleonomic pressure of
natural selection". Thus the ritualized unit promotes better signal
function; it is more readily understood.

Individual Variation

Individual variation means, simply, that no two individuals are
exactly alike. Countless variations may occur which in no way
affect survival. In kinesics these variances are interpreted as

ideokinesic features in the individual's behavioral repertoire, a blend of genetic predisposition, muscular-skeletal build, and personal life experience.

RELEVANT PRINCIPLES FROM ETHOLOGY

Within this framework we may consider some concepts from ethology as they pertain to human nonverbal behavior. Ethology is based on the principle that all behavior operates upon a panhuman base which is basically biologic and operates largely out-of-awareness -- unlearned and nondifferentiating. Upon this foundation a complex of learned, differentiated behaviors form; they are influenced mainly by experience and culture and are usually consciously performed. Finally, atop this second level are the ideosyncratic features unique to the individual, determined partially by genetic endowment along with his particular body rhythm, significant personal experiences (particularly in infancy and childhood), physical health, and related factors.

Fixed-Action Patterns

The fundamental behavior patterns serve an adaptive function because each pattern is performed in an appropriate situation. They have been termed endogenous or fixed-action patterns, 'endogenous' referring to their remarkable independence of external stimulation. Rather, internal motivation appears to provide their energy. These basic patterns are important because they underlie everything else, form the basis on which learning occurs, and on which other behaviors form; and they are genetically determined and exist in levels ranging from tiny micro units to large macro structures.

Appetitive Behavior

Because the source of motivation, or energy, is internal, it accumulates when no stimuli for appropriate discharge is available. The individual then becomes more active -- not because he is searching for stimuli, but to increase his chances of encountering it. In ethological terms this is appetitive behavior, first noted and described by Craig (5). It is thus a "purposive searching." The range of appetitive behavior is enormous, from restless pacing to abstract achievements in the realms of learning and insight (10) -- we "search" for knowledge, for answers. This is a most useful concept in the understanding of kinesic behavior and its role in the communicational process.

Imprinting and IRM

Another ethological concept applicable to kinesic behavior is that of imprinting, originally noted by Konrad Lorenz. It indicates a predisposed, genetically prompted desire, at a particular time, to define environmental elements as respondents to one's needs. Lorenz discovered the phenomenon while studying geese: newborn goslings, within hours after birth, accepted the first sighted moving object as their mother; this primitive "identification" continued and became permanent. The role of imprinting in human learning acquisition has not been fully determined, but it definitely plays a role in the reception and assimilation of environmental cues. Lorenz later expanded the concept to that of the Innate Releasing Mechanism (IRM), a signal, which when perceived "releases" a sequence, or set, of behaviors or a behavioral pattern. The IRM is operative in a number of human motor patterns; some are learned and culturally-determined. Spitz has utilized the IRM to explain the smiling response in infants (13, page 95). A particular configuration within the face perceived by the infant serves as the releaser of the smiling response. Interestingly, the "triggering" stimulus -- in this instance an area centered about the eyes of the person seen by the infant -- must be in motion as must the mother object of Lorenz' goslings. The significance here is the infant's response to movement coupled with holding and physical contact by another human; it reiterates the complex interaction involved in all forms of life. This infant response presupposes a dyadic reciprocal response between infant and mother (or surrogate), laying the foundation for subsequent relationships. Spitz emphasizes this mutuality of "give and take, its single elements constantly changing and shifting" (13, page 96).

Releasers

The concepts of releaser and releasing mechanism serve to correlate many otherwise seemingly unrelated behaviors and causal relationships. Because of our conceptual, abstracting abilities, operative releasing mechanisms may be seen as the precursors of symbols. The Christian cross or the Star of David, a national flag, the exposed female breast in American culture are only a few examples which can release a series of mental abstractions bearing significance to the individual perceiving them. Even a word can

serve as a releaser -- limbo, Ivy League, Archie Bunker. A word
may release differing sets of abstractions: "the bench" may signify
judge and judicial system to one while it may relate to the sports
world for another, as "on the bench" or "being benched. "

These, then, are fundamental concepts from ethology concerning
basic instinctual motor patterns with their own autonomous appetite
and internal source of energy. When adequate stimulation is with-
held, central nervous potential is accumulated. The endogenous
production of these basic behavior patterns is closely interrelated
with physiological processes. These, and related concepts, have
been developed by ethologists following the pioneering work by
Darwin on expressive behavior.

DARWIN: THREE PRINCIPLES

Darwin proposed three principles in his effort to explain the expression of emotions. These are useful in understanding many nonverbal behaviors.

1. The principle of serviceable-associated habits consists of
need-meeting behaviors for the individual. Some acts, at first performed consciously, have gradually been converted to reflex action
due to the influence of habit and association, thus becoming part and
parcel of our basic biologic structure. We "jump" when startled,
we back off quickly when confronted unexpectedly by something
associated with harm or danger. And as we jump away we inevitably
close our eyes, or at least blink, as a protective mechanism. These
are reflex-actions, self preservative, and modified to serve a specific function. So any sensation, whether related to threat or desire,
has led to the evolvement of a related movement; over time that
movement comes to be elicited when the same or an analogous situation occurs. Some of these movements are performed with full consciousness, others are partially repressed. In either case, their
performance is highly expressive.

2. The principle of antithesis is a particularly intriguing concept as it applies to human nonverbal behavior. This principle refers to the involuntary performance of movements due to certain
conflicting "states of mind. " Darwin cites shrugging of the shoulders
as an antithetical movement -- perhaps an unconscious wish to attack or deal forcibly with a situation, superseded by a conscious or

preconscious sense of impotence or ineffectiveness in dealing with it.
Some of these antithetical patterns have become basic motor patterns.
Darwin states, "As the performance of ordinary movements of an
opposite kind, under opposite impulses of the will, has become ha-
bitual.... so when actions of one kind have been firmly associated
with any sensation or emotion, it appears natural that actions of a
directly opposite kind, though of no use, should be unconsciously
performed through habit and association, under the influence of a
directly opposite sensation or emotion" (6). One may recall seeing
a guest leaving a party comment to the hostess, "I had a marvelous
time," while his head moves back and forth, a "negative head nod."
Or a student may remark to his professor, "Gee, I really enjoyed
this course," while his head and eye movements contradict his statement.

  3. The principle of actions due to the constitution of the nervous system relates to central arousal states. As an example,
trembling serves no useful purpose but is a reaction to the direct
excitation and action of the neural network. Trembling is initiated
by a variety of excitatory stimuli: fear, anger, pleasure. We speak
of "shivers of delight"; there are also shivers of fear, threat,
anxiety. Darwin proposed that "any strong excitement of the nervous system interrupts the steady flow of nerve-force to the muscles," resulting in trembling (6, page 68). Anger and, more markedly, rage lead to nonverbal expression in the appearance of dilated
nostrils, clenched teeth and fists, labored breathing. This third
principle preceded later physiological findings concerning functional
states of central arousal.

  The genius of Darwin's contributions is realized in micro research of filmed behavior, the frame-by-frame study of movement.
Fleeting facial expressions, almost imperceptible at normal speed,
are often clearly delineated at the micro level. He noted the movements of lips and mouth during a state of rage or disgust -- "We
still uncover the canine tooth, on one side, when we sneer at or
defy anyone, and we uncover all our teeth when furiously enraged"
(6, page 247). A transient sneer may sometimes be seen in micro
study of a film segment, merging into another expression; there may
be no apparent correlation with the verbal content. The act of
frowning, Darwin noted, was acquired during infancy when pain,
anger, or distress occurred; thus it approached the reaction of
screaming. There are fleeting "frown-expressions" in the range of
human facial expressions, too. Darwin noted that frowning also

serves as a shade in difficult or intense vision -- in bright sunlight, for example, or in deep concentration. He considered this to be a protective device evolved as a result of our upright posture. Perhaps Darwin's greatest contribution was his recognition of the range of human emotional states, assigning man a unique position, with vast potentials, in his environment.

THE EMOTIONS

Their Genesis in Infancy

This "range of emotional states" adds another dimension to our consideration of nonverbal behaviors. To realize the genesis of these states and their expressive potential, we may consider a continuum ranging from instinctual neural patterns to the various emotions, or affects, as descriptive of the various subjective feeling states. We may begin by considering that, at birth, the infant is totally dependent upon the environment and caregivers within it. But he moves, primarily with uncoordinated motion of hands, arms, legs, feet. By the age of three months he has achieved a greater range of movement and thence proceeds to further stages of coordinated movement. The infant at first exists in an undifferentiated world, unable to distinguish self from others or the internal from the external -- it is an "objectless surround." He is aware of comfort as opposed to discomfort, signaling the latter vocally (with healthy lungs) and with increased motor activity. He can respond to tactile and auditory stimuli, noted in the startle reflex -- a jerking movement produced by a loud sound or similar stimuli. To protect him from a flood of undifferentiated stimuli, a stimulus barrier exists. It continues to serve this protective function until the emerging ego can begin to take over the process. This rudimentary ego appears at about the age of three months.

The neonate experiences pleasure when he is warm, dry, fed, and generally cared for, his needs at that particular time met. He experiences unpleasure when a state of tension exists due to some source of discomfort. The state of pleasure leads to the establishment of object: "another" provides appropriate care. This primal dyad leads to subsequent object-relationships. The condition of unpleasure is centered in the loss of the object; at that moment tension rises. The smiling response relates to anticipation of a state of pleasure; crying is the precursor of increased tension and

a state of discomfort. These opposing states may be described in
yet another way -- gratification as opposed to frustration, or passivity vs. activity.

It is important to realize the significance of the mother-infant
interrelationship at this pre-verbal level. It forms the basis for
(1) subsequent object-relationships; (2) the emergence of affects;
and (3) the organization of perception which is learned, coordinated,
and integrated through the experience of object relations and carries
an implicit charge of some related affect or "emotional state" in
cognitive-abstractive processes (13, page 84). So perception,
which we will consider later, is correlated with interpersonal relations and with emotions.

Emotions in Infancy Related to Sign-Signal-Symbol

Another point to be clarified here is the differentiation among
communicational modes. Adults communicate via verbal and kinesic
symbol, but the mother-infant dyad repertoire is that of sign-signal
(13, pages 132-133). The infant's mode is that of sign only, a percept as it pertains to an object or situation and directed to the environment at large. The mother may respond verbally, but her
main mode is that of signal which is a directed, volitional mode. As
the infant's psyche develops and matures he will move from sign to
signal to symbol, but he will retain remnants of each in his total
behavioral repertoire throughout life.

Emotions in Infancy Related to Adult Patterns

The rooting response, in combination with sucking, is the only
directed behavior at birth; all other is random. The clutch reflex,
closing the hand when the palm is stimulated, is present but non-
directed. By the age of four months the grasping reflex is becoming
subordinated to higher-level functions. By nine months the thumb
is fully opposed and grasp is effected with greater accuracy. As
developmental patterns continue and motor behaviors become in-
creasingly coordinated, these earliest archaic movements are gradually introjected into behavior patterns as vestiges of their original
form. Bowlby (1) states, "All remain in fresh combinations when
the adult repertoire comes to mature.... Like old soldiers, infantile
instinctual responses never die."

In an excellent research study utilizing film frame-by-frame analysis, Dr. Felix Loeb found that a particular adult "mechanically purposeless grasp-like movement" was identical in both micro-motor pattern and range of duration to those pressor movements per-formed by infants while nursing. Loeb states, "Thus, this grasp-like movement pattern, which was first found to occur regularly with a specific class of meaning in adult humans, appears to have a phylogenetically inherited, biological basis" (9). Of added signifi-cance is another finding by Loeb (9, page 6) -- that the adult move-ment "regularly occurred in lexical contexts containing a specific ideational content which Freud, and later Spitz, attributed to the nursing situation." These lexical messages ranged from reference to a person, object, or thought -- getting in or close to someone or their mind -- or negation of these situations -- out or away from them.

Loeb refers to Spitz' comment that rooting behavior occurs when the newborn has developed "neither consciousness nor perception.... is definitely not a volitional signal or a directed communication.... it is an indicator, perceived by the environment and taken for a communication" (14). With later formation of object relations, rooting behavior will change function and will thus become a commu-nicative pattern.

A related study by Dr. Donald Coleman describes the homologous relationship of adult action patterns in an awake state of "resistant remembering" to a cluster of action patterns performed by the in-fant as he awakens from sleep: sucking movements, grasping, yawning and stretching, mouthing and vocalizations (4). A sequence of states in the infant's sleep-wakefulness continuum is markedly similar to the adult sleep patterns noted in recent Rapid Eye Move-ment (REM) sleep research. There is first a drowsy, inactive period similar to the adult hypnogogic phase. This is followed by alternating periods of active sleep with rapid eye movements, and periods of quiet sleep characterized by regular, shallow breathing and reduced motoric activity. A pertinent observation by Coleman relates to the transitional period from the last phase of active sleep into an alert, exploring phase of wakefulness. At this point the described cluster of action patterns is performed by the infant. Clinical observations have supported Coleman's hypothesis that these action patterns would be observed in awake adults when at-tempting, but resisting, the recall of a memory, dream, or similar image. Adult behaviors such as stretching, yawning, grasping, hand-to-mouth movements seem to occur as one "rummages through one's body" . . . "regression in the service of resistance" (4, page 13). Vestigial traces of infantile action patterns are, indeed, retained throughout life.

As the basic motor behaviors evolve into behavior patterns, so the undifferentiated state of the neonate yields to emergent perception and affective experience, the foundation for the "range of emotional states" noted by Darwin. Emotions also have a communicative quality; expressed nonverbally they serve a signal function of needs, wishes, desires, impulses. These behaviors might be termed affective language and Brierley (2) notes that "Affect language is older than speech." In the newborn, "sensing" is centered in the autonomic nervous system and is primarily visceral. Gradually, as maturation proceeds, this sensing becomes more localized, centered in the cortex, and manifested in cognitive processes (13).

Adult Affective States

Adult affective, or emotional, states present a spectrum of feeling states. We convey information about our emotions via several modes: lexical; kinesic movements, gestures, and postures; and visceral changes -- one's face becomes pale or flushed, we tremble, or muscle tonus increases, we may become "bathed in perspiration" or notice that the mouth and lips become dry.

Affective States As Means of Communication

Rapaport describes three components of affect: (1) "affect discharge channels" present from birth, (2) their subsequent modification into "affect charges," and (3) their development into "affect signals" as emotional processes become communicative devices (11). So as the infant proceeds from sign to signal to symbol in one communicational mode, he similarly proceeds through corresponding developmental stages of the conveying of emotion.

The Inner Subjective State

There is also a covert world of emotional content, the subjective affect states, which William James has described as "the sort of unuttered inner atmosphere in which (one's) consciousness

lives alone," an inner personal tone (8). We may consciously realize
feelings of shame, guilt, happiness, pride, despair, to name but a
few of the limitless possibilities. Or they may exist in our preconscious like dim, hovering shadows, or they may be denied or
relegated to the repressed. There is a complex interrelationship,
not yet fully understood, of the subjective "inner sensing" with the
overt communicational expression of emotion and their correlation
with neurophysiological mechanisms. The organism seeks a state
of equilibrium among these states via adaptive mechanisms, as described by W. B. Cannon in 1929 (3) and later by Hans Selye (1950),
identified by the latter as the General Adaptation Syndrome (G. A. S.)
(12).

Inclusion of these various factors is necessary if one is to
realize the totality of the communicational process and the role of
nonverbal behaviors within it. For example, while a young man is
talking to a friend, he is also assuming a posture, gesturing, feeling
happy or sad, enthused or bored, worried or nonchalant. And his
heartbeat may be steady, rapid, or slow; his blood pressure low or
elevated (for him). He may or may not be consciously aware of his
subjective state at that moment. If he is, he may mention, "I feel
great," or "I'm miserable." He may not verbalize a feeling of depression, but it may be conveyed kinesically -- folded, sagging
posture, corners of the mouth turned down, retarded gait. This may
be a reactive depression -- his date stood him up, he's flunking a
course, he has financial worries. The meaning of the incident for
the young man reflects its affective charge and what it symbolizes
to him -- the broken date perhaps reactivating feelings of rejection,
loss, or inadequacy; the course failure a blow to his need for performance and achievement; the concern over finances threatening
his need for security, status, control, depending on whatever money
per se symbolizes to him. Or this may be an endogenous depression,
perhaps triggered by some physiological complex. In any event, his
kinesic behaviors are an integral part of his adaptational state and
of the total communicational process.

SUMMARY

The organized complexity of nonverbal communication begins to
emerge as we examine these concepts from the biological sciences,
providing the "building blocks" for an understanding of the panhuman,
basic, and instinctual behavior patterns. These basic motor
sequences constitute the foundation for other evolved sequences

while retaining their own significant communicational functions.
Because of their regularity, many of these patterns serve as releasing mechanisms, eliciting an appropriate response; yet they
also serve as expressions of various emotional feeling states. In
toto they comprise the biologic matrix of human expressive behavior.

REFERENCES

1. John Bowlby, "The nature of the child's tie to his mother," Intl. J. Psychoanal., 39, 350-373, as noted in Ref. 9, 1958.

2. M. Brierly, "Affects in theory and practice," Intl. J. Psychoanal., 18, 265, 1937.

3. Walter B. Cannon. Bodily Changes in Pain, Hunger, Fear and Rage. New York: Appleton, 1929.

4. Donald J. Coleman, "The dream of Rorschach: A note on action in the forgetting of dreams," unpublished manuscript, 1968.

5. W. Craig, "Appetites and aversions as constituents of instincts," Biol. Bull., 34, 91-107, 1918.

6. Charles Darwin. The Expression of the Emotions in Man and Animals. Chicago: Univ. of Chicago Press, 1965 (orig. ed., 1872), p. 65.

7. Julian Huxley. Ritualization of Behavior. Philosophical Transactions of the Royal Society of London, Series B, Vol. 251. London: The Royal Society, 1966, Introduction.

8. William James, "The gospel of relaxation," in Essays on Faith and Morals. New York: Longmans Green & Co., 1949, p. 241.

9. Felix F. Loeb, "Grasping: The psychoanalytic implications of a recurrent behavior pattern," unpublished manuscript, 1969, p. 6.

10. Konrad Lorenz. On Aggression. New York: Harcourt Brace & World, 1966, p. 53.

11. David Rapaport. The Structure of Psychoanalytic Theory: A Systematizing Attempt. Psychological Issues, Monograph #6. New York: International Univ. Press, 1960.

12. Hans Selye. <u>The Stress of Life</u>. New York: McGraw-Hill, 1956.

13. Rene A. Spitz. <u>The First Year of Life</u>. New York: International Universities, 1965.

14. Rene A. Spitz. <u>No and Yes</u>. New York: International Univ. Press, 1957, p. 33 as noted in Ref. 9.

THREE

THE LEARNED BEHAVIORS

PERCEPTION

Our pursuit into the nature of communication as it relates to nonverbal behaviors leads now to a general consideration of several
interrelated factors. As the infant proceeds through subsequent
stages of development, learned patterns of behavior become established upon the previously described biologic base. A gradual awareness of the environment begins as the infant emerges from the totally
dependent state of the newborn. He distinguishes objects and people,
for perception is evolving. Unpleasure vs. a kind of neutral state
have become separate, so that pleasure is equated with gratification
and unpleasure is analogous with threat -- an imminent fear of needs
not being met. The infant first perceives the emotional significance
of a situation -- meaning precedes object in the development of perception. At about the age of four months there is a shift from passive
relationship with the environment to the beginning of a more active
interchange. However, this kind of pre-object activity relates only
to those environmental objects holding meaning for the infant, "action-
objects" as described by Werner (19).

But "action-objects" lack continuity, permanence. Both the form
and the content of thought vary with age, so as maturation proceeds
a rudimentary gestalt or frame of reference emerges. Piaget notes
that "perceptual regulations" occur at about the age of three years,
along with other cognitive developments (10). This signifies the
selection and ordering of "sense data" in regard to self and environment; it is strongly influenced by family, ethnic and social class,
individual and interpersonal experience and the linking of affects to
these experiences. From these beginnings "sensing" one's world
and interpreting it develops into a highly skilled and rapidly performed process. It is through one's perceptual mode that major
themes, analogs, become patterned in personality -- "Who can be
trusted?" "Better be careful 'cause you never know....," "I might
be left out..or rejected," "It may be tough but I can handle it."
Each of us has a set of a few such major statements, highly organized
and integrated into our personality structure. They are a correlate
of our inner perception of self with our outer-directed view of the
world and persons in it, evolved from our unique life experiences.

Perception necessarily involves a decision process. No one can possibly handle all incoming stimuli, so a selection process occurs, designating the choice of material meaningful to the individual. Thus there is a screening out of much potential information in the building of a percept. While this screening process occurs on an individual basis, it must conform generally to the culturally-shared percepts, both implicit and explicit, if communication is to be functional. When individual perceptions extend beyond the proscribed range of the accepted norm, extrusion by the group will most likely occur and the individual will be labelled deviant.

CULTURE

While the basic perceptual skills are developing, other new patterns are also becoming established through the process of initial learning. A large part of this learning process, particularly in the preschool years, is determined by the culture of the child and his family. The teaching of culture is effected through the child's socialization experiences, and the family serves as primary enculturalizer of the small child. In daily contact with family members, participating as an integral member of the family system, the child acquires and internalizes a vast range of attitudes, values, linguistic and kinesic behaviors. Again, the social class of the family, its ethnic and racial origins, geographic location, and even degree of family stability, are some of the biosocial variables relating to the complex of this cultural milieu. The child learns also by means of parental instruction, by their system of reward and punishment, and through imitative play. The derived systems of the culture, including its games, jokes, and other forms of relaxation; its drama, music, folklore, myths -- all contribute to this enculturalizing process.

Every human society, regardless of circumstance or locale, has evolved some type of culture. Primitive tribes have been found to possess highly elaborate cultures. In fact, without culture there could probably be no "human nature" as we know it. Murdoch has succinctly defined culture as "systems of collective habits," a compressed but viable definition of a most significant environmental influence (9). Social transmission of these behavioral clusters, or "collective habits," is effected through the family and other primary identification groups.

Cultures are not stationary entities; there are historical shifts within them over time, comparable to the biological phylogenetic changes previously noted (Chapter 2). There are also simultaneous variations within each group and subgroup -- shifts, blends, admixtures -- due to the multidimensional nature of human interaction. Thus "culture borrowing" may occur with a resultant culture diffusion. A complex society such as exists in America today has many subcultures, each with its distinctive set of creeds, values, and related attributes representing stylized differences. There is a range, too, in the degree of separation and individuation of the subgroup from its larger counterpart. The degree of separateness serves as a determining factor in the extent to which these distinguishing differences will remain intact or will become amalgamated with other cultural factors which the child may encounter.

Yet, despite these diversities, the culture exists as a prime influencer of the young child, and this culture is essentially a coherent, integrated system with pattern and order; it is not just a miscellany of whimsical practices, habits, and random beliefs. Rather, it comprises a cluster of values and attitudes in combination with other learned behaviors, linguistic characteristics, and kinesic mannerisms, which form the bulwark of the child's enculturalization experience.

The foundation for role perception and role acquisition is found here. More particularly, the cultural definition of what is masculine and what is feminine evolves early; it pertains to body movement, posture, and the general nature of kinesic sexual behavior. "Gender signals" evolve from the cultural body code learned and introjected during childhood. This sexual differentiation begins almost at birth. Most Americans tend to "think blue" for boys and "pink" for girls. Infant girls are usually handled more gently. We tend to establish a different emotional atmosphere around male and female infants, and the differentiation continues through childhood. This role transmission is consistent with the value orientation of the cultural group. Spiegel has termed the process "role induction" as applied to family role conflict (17); a very similar inductive process occurs in culturally-determined sexual role discrimination. Later modification via subsequent experience may, of course, occur to some degree, but the basic identification process occurs in the preschool years.

LANGUAGE

Essential to any culture is its language, the spoken and written format of communication. Smith notes that the linguistic system of a culture interrelates with the other systems of that culture and also reflects the content of these systems, thus operating on a "culturological" level (16). A culture evolves its concept of reality as it is generally perceived by that group; the nature of its language reflects the interplay of its mythology, ethics, customs, rituals, and functional skills. There is the deep structure of a language, closely related to meaning, established by early rules of its generation. Surface structure alludes to those later transformations, the language as it is actually heard and used. Subcultures further vary the surface structure to coincide with their perceptual schema.

Speech Behavior and the Whorfian Hypothesis

Thus, speech behavior is embedded in the total complex of learned behaviors and is closely related to the percepts of a culture. This theme is well stated in the Whorfian hypothesis, a significant construct which refers to language being an active determinant of what is perceived and thought. People think and act in terms of the classifications they use (their language); thus they project meaning onto features of the world as they perceive it. Benjamin Lee Whorf conceived of forms in a linguistic system placing finite limits on the range of available "categories" and hence on the degree of perceptual differentiation established. He described our living in a "noumenal world" of complex, patterned relationships (20). So people of different cultures not only speak different languages but also inhabit different sensory worlds!

The umwelt, as conceived by ethologist von Uexkull, in a similar manner refers to the environment, and particularly spatial relationships within it, as it is perceived, the phenomenal or self-world (18). For we seek harmony in our perceptual schema, akin to the "cognitive consistency" aptly investigated by the social psychologists. These factors, in turn, relate also to variations in kinesic behaviors, for all are interwoven in our behavioral gestalten. We move in our perceptual-linguistic modality.

Linguistics

Linguistics is the study of unique properties of speech behavior as, for example, (a) voice qualities and (b) vocalizations, the function of sounds within a system of sounds. There are specialized areas of linguistic study: its development (Historical Linguistics), the structure and pattern of language (Structural Linguistics), as well as its relationship to other languages (Comparative Linguistics). The Sanskrit word mata becomes mater in Latin, mutter in German, mere in French, mother in English. The Greek and Persian terms are similar.

Pike's detailed studies of language (11) as a portion of human behavior led to his constructs of -etic and -emic, coined from the words phonetic and phonemic. The -etic views all cultures and languages from outside their systems, a physical description, while -emic refers to the structure of behavioral components within the system, as well as the function they serve. Franz Boaz, Leonard Bloomfield, Edward Sapir, and other noted linguists developed sophisticated methods for the analysis of discrete linguistic phenomena.

Sapir, particularly interested in the microcultural aspects of language as it relates to personality, delineated five levels of speech behavior (13). An understanding of them may enhance our awareness of the impact which speech behavior effects in our perception of others. It may encourage us to look at our self-presentation via spoken communication. And we may acknowledge the close relationship they bear to kinesic behaviors. The five levels include the following:

Voice Quality. The characteristic element of one's vocalizations: resonant, thin, mellow, flat; determined partially by glottis control. Sapir notes that we may "see" a person as sentimental, brusque, cruel, etc., our judgment based in large part on his voice quality.

Voice Dynamics. This relates to intonation, the rise and fall of vocalizations; speech rhythms (even, jerky, smooth, or choppy), speed (slow, drawling, fast, staccato). Pitch, range, stress, and inflection are additional factors.

Pronunciation. There is a range of acceptable variation in speech utterance, and ideosyncratic pronunciation must be within this range if one is to be understood. The use of lip and tongue, as well as glottis and articulation control contribute to dialectic and individually unique pronunciation. This is the "distinct timbre" of one's speech behavior. It may vary according to context, Sapir notes, so that 'tiny' may become 'teeny' when talking to a small child.

Vocabulary. The choice of words used to express oneself is a significant variable, an expression of larger units of percepts and analogs. There is the "social" vocabulary of the cultural group and also "personal" word choices. We may choose words because we like them or their sound; we may avoid using others because they annoy or even frighten us. Our associations to words are intricate and complex.

Style. Is there a flair to one's language behavior or is it dull? Does one tend to redundancy or is he "to the point"? Here, too, may be found analogs of personality. "The box dropped" conveys a meaning of displaced fault or explanation; "I dropped the box" indicates responsibility for the act. "I have to go to the library" is not synonymous with "I'm going to the library."

Smith and Trager analyzed phonemic intonation in combination with pitch and terminal junctures in American speech (15). Stress structures vary and the variance may alter meaning. "Con-duct" differs in connotation from "con-duct"; "the white-house" creates an image quite different from "the white-house." This is the accentual feature of speech behavior. American English is described as a four-stress language -- primary, secondary, tertiary, and weak. Stress points organize into stress patterns, creating a rhythm unique to the individual. Terminal junctures refer to voice pitch at the completion of a phrase or sentence: it may rise, drop, or be held steady.

These elements, in combination, have been termed paralanguage, or paralinguistic elements of articulated thought. Birdwhistell (4) and Scheflen (14) define the function of paralanguage as a means of reducing ambiguity by the provision of supplemental information.

Condon (7) explains it within the context of micro-analogues of personality and a means of cross-monitoring, or cross-referencing,
interpersonal messages. Paralanguage actually performs all these
functions if we but become attuned to its rich array of meaning.

KINESICS AS RELATED TO THE LEARNED BEHAVIORS

Parakinesic phenomena interrelate with these paralinguistic
behaviors. They are "non-lexical modifiers" contributing to the
communicational gestalt. And they must be considered within the
context of "the whiles" (Chapter 1) to be understood; isolated as discrete units they have no meaning. We must also distinguish between
prekinesic phenomena -- the pan-human, biological motor patterns --
and kinesic behaviors -- the learned, adapted units.

Gestures are kinemorphs bound to a higher level of kinesic
constructions as "stem forms" in language are always related to
more complex units. Neither gesture nor stem form has meaning in
itself; each must be considered within the context of the larger order. Birdwhistell notes two main classes of parakinesic behaviors.
Motion qualifiers apply to small segments of kinemorphic behavior.
They include intensity, duration, and range. Intensity is the degree
of muscle tonus involved in production of a kine, kinemorph, or
kinemorphic construction. This may vary from tense to lax with
varying intermediate states. Duration is the time involved in performance of any of the above units, from overly brief to an extended
period, as compared with the behavioral norm. Range is the extent
of motion involved in performance of a kinesic unit, on a continuum
from narrow to broad.

Action modifiers refer to gross body movements. They include
the general rhythm of movement; the degree of integration and con-
gruency among body parts; emphasis upon, or avoidance of, a particular body area; velocity of body movement -- fast or slow; and
the degree of body congruence as it relates to the context (5).

Parakinesic behaviors also include motion markers which often
serve as punctuation to the verbal content. Arlow has noted four
ways of relating nonverbal and verbal communication which are
particularly applicable to kinesic markers. The nonverbal element
may serve as punctuation by either emphasizing or denying the verbal content; it may serve as a glossary -- explaining, translating;

it may be a "marginal annotation," a running commentary; or the automatisms may be eruptions of "totally dissociated, though highly organized, coexistent mental activity "(1).

Birdwhistell relates these kinesic markers to their "derived functions," the observable behaviors which can be isolated and interpreted. Such derived functions would include signals of anticipated interruption or termination of verbal comments. They consist of behaviors such as head, hand, and foot nods; eye focus shifts; raised eyebrows; area signals such as "pointing" with the head or head sweeps and hand gestures or hand sweeps as distance signals. There are also "pronominal reference markers" emphasizing verbalized content relating to I, we, they, it, with related head, finger, or hand points or sweeps (4, page 223). When these markers occur upon completion of an utterance they are termed "terminal junctures."

Paralinguistic and parakinesic behaviors are intricately and mutually related. They are culturally molded and, while understood within the cultural group, may be misinterpreted by others. Americans and Europeans are familiar with a pointing of the index finger as a kinesic punctuation marker; East Africans point only with the chin and lips. Eye-blinks of the American male are more rapid than those of the Arab male, whose langorous eye-blinks contribute to a different facial configuration-of-change set. Inhabitants of Greece nod the head vertically to signal yes, as do Americans, but the Greek no is conveyed by a backward jerking of the head, lifting the face and brow, and with the eyes often closed. Americans usually raise the head slightly upon completion of a statement when an answer is expected; this signal, readily recognized in the American culture, thus serves as an elicitor of some response.

Efron's thorough comparison study of the gestures used by Southern Italians and those used by East European Jews (8) illustrates the marked gestural differences that exist. He found that the Italian group illustrates gesturally the "objects" of their thinking activity, which he termed "the referents," while the Jewish group was more likely to use a gestural notation of the "process" of the verbalized material, e.g., the reference. Members of both groups were recent immigrants to New York City from their homelands. Efron noted that the immigrant Jews kept the elbow close to the body, moving it within only a narrow range, and utilized angular

zigzag motions, often like a figure O. The Southern Italians sat
farther apart than members of the Eastern European group, possibly
to allow space for their larger gestures. Observations of second
and third generation Italian-Americans who have maintained a close
ethnic affiliation indicate their retention of frequent expansive arm
and hand movements, and the unique four-finger closed-hand position
with thumb resting against the third finger; it is thrust out toward
the listener   or merely into space with quick, jabbing flicks.

An interesting conclusion drawn by Efron relates to the loss of
traditional culture-specific gestures by members of both groups as
they were assimilated into the American culture. The more assimilated they became, the fewer Jewish or Italian gestural traits
they retained -- an example of culture diffusion as it relates to kinesic behavior. Efron also noted the "hybrid gestures" of persons
exposed to more than one culture and the "gesture bilingualism" of
a bilingual person -- he tends to utilize the gestural mannerisms of
the language he speaks. Certainly these observations demonstrate
the high degree of organization in our communicational behavior.

A detailed series of studies described by Rosalie Cohen (6) point
to differing conceptual styles and related language use by children
from low- and middle-income American homes. Semantic feature
analysis of the lexicon utilized by the lower-income children revealed time perception as a series of discrete moments rather than a
continuum, perception of self in the center of social space as opposed
to being relative to others, causality of events being specific rather
multiple in origin. These differences in cognitive style are independent of native ability, reflecting only a variation in conceptual modes.
"Ghetto language" also reflects the social climate of that population,
a unique linguistic signal system, which tends to be self-assertive
and directive, using language in a manipulative way -- a mirror of
the ghetto's perceptual and cultural world. Basil Bernstein (2)
studied the speech structure of lower and middle class English children and found that the former consistently used a restricted code,
while the latter employed elaborate coding, i.e., fewer personal
pronouns, more intricate sentence structure, greater variety of con-
junctions, more logical speech sequence.

Black English has come to be recognized as a dialect with its
own grammar, vocabulary, and unique phonetics. It is a blend of
three centuries' usage: bits of English picked up from slave masters,
portions of native African dialects (jazz and banjo are both African

words) retained over time, and a variety of combined forms. The
result is a "creolization" or pidgin language native to no one, generally used in a limited range of situations by blacks. "Switching" has
often been utilized by blacks as a resolution of the problem -- using
the intimate dialect in the home and cultural group, speaking stan-
dard English in other social situations.

There is also a unique rhythmicity to the body movement of
blacks. Kinesic research indicates that blacks body movement is
often "syncopated," a seeming 4/4 head rhythm juxtaposed with a
6/8 body, hand, and arm rhythm. White Americans appear to maintain a 4/4 rhythm in both the head and trunk areas. These variations
in movement merit further study, for they may assist in enabling
interracial communication and understanding. Blacks use frequent
circular hand and arm gestures; whites tend to exercise linear movements and gestures. Arm and hand movements of blacks are often
rapid with considerable micro movements of the hands and fingers --
they dart out quickly as a black gesticulates. There are, of course,
ideokinesic variations in addition to historically determined variations.

SYMBOLS

So, as the learned behaviors build on the pan-human base,
differences appear. The triage of acquired traits -- perception,
culture, language -- and their interrelationship with kinesic behaviors -- all contribute to our humanness if we can but overcome
our "blind spots" and prejudices. None of the features in this com-
pendium of environmental variables would be possible without man's
potential for abstract representation, wherein one object, idea, percept may stand for another, due to some shared attribute as it is
perceived. Disguised emotional meanings attached to the original
object are often carried over to its substitute; condensed experiences
and feelings may also be attached to the replacement. Without this
remarkable attribute we could never have attained any degree of
civilized state for, as Sahlins (12) has noted, "Spontaneous teamwork
presupposes symboling."

Von Bertalanffy suggests that the new, emerging science of man
must include two key terms: symbolism and system. We live in a
universe of pattern and order -- the biological system -- and also
"in a symbolic world of language, thought, social entities, money,
science, religion, art, what have you, and the objective world...."

from trivial surroundings to books, cars, cities and bombs, are
materializations of symbolic activities (3). Thus, translation of
experience into other symbolic forms may serve to enhance social
and cultural variations. All of these factors in toto contribute to
variations in kinesic behavior and to the complexity of human communication.

REFERENCES

1. J. A. Arlow, "Motor behavior as nonverbal communicat-ion," paper read at Fall Meeting, American Psychoanalytic Association, New York, December, 1968. In J. Amer. Psycho-anal. Assoc., 17, 960-961, 1969.

2. Basil Bernstein, "Elaborate and restricted codes: Their origin and some consequences," in The Ethnography of Communi-cation, (J. J. Gumperz and D. Hymes, eds.). Special publication of Amer. Anthropol., 66, Part 2, #6, 1964.

3. Ludwig von Bertalanffy. Organismic Psychology and Sy-stems Theory. Barre, Massachusetts: Clark Univ. Press and Barre Publishers, 1968, p. 13.

4. Ray L. Birdwhistell. Kinesics and Context. Philadelphia: Univ. of Pennsylvania Press, 1970.

5. Ray L. Birdwhistell, "Paralanguage: Twenty-five years after Sapir," in Lectures on Experimental Psychiatry (Henry W. Brosin, ed.). Pittsburgh: Univ. of Pittsburgh Press, 1961.

6. Rosalie A. Cohen, "Conceptual styles, culture conflict and nonverbal tests of intelligence," Amer. Anthropol., 71, 828-856, 1969.

7. William Condon, personal communication.

8. David Efron. Gesture and Environment. New York: King's Crown Press, 1942.

9. George P. Murdoch, "How culture changes," in Man, Cul-ture and Society (Harry P. Shipiro, ed.). Oxford: The University Press, 1956.

10. Jean Piaget. Les mechanismes perceptifs. Paris: Presses Universitaires de France, 1968.

11. Kenneth L. Pike. Language in Relation to a Unified Theory of the Structure of Human Behavior. The Hague: Mouton & Co., 1967.

12. Marshall D. Sahlins, in The Evolution of Man's Capacity for Culture, Symposium (1957), arranged by J. N. Spuhler, Detroit: Wayne State Univ. Press, 1959, p. 64.

13. Edward Sapir. Selected Writings (David G. Mandelbaum, ed.). Berkeley: Univ. of California Press, 1949, pp. 536-543.

14. A. E. Scheflen, "The significance of posture in communication systems," Psychiatry, 27, 316-331, 1964.

15. H. L. Smith, Jr. and G. L. Trager. An Outline of English Structure. Norman, Oklahoma: Battenburg, 1951.

16. Henry Lee Smith. Linguistic Science (Inglis Lecture, 1954). Cambridge: Harvard Univ. Press, 1956, p. 5.

17. John Spiegel, "The resolution of role conflict within the family," in Sourcebook in Abnormal Psychology (Leslie Y. Rabkin and John E. Carr, eds.). Boston: Houghton Mifflin, 1957, p. 123.

18. Jakob Johann von Uexkull, cited in Instinctive Behavior (Claire Schiller, ed.). New York: International Universities Press, 1957, p. 5.

19. Heinz Werner. Comparative Psychology of Mental Development (revised ed.). Chicago: Follett, 1948.

20. Benjamin Lee Whorf. Language, Thought and Reality. Published jointly by the Technology Press of M.I.T. (Boston) and J. Wiley & Sons (New York), 1956, p. 247.

FOUR

AGGRESSION AND NONVERBAL COMMUNICATION

DEFINITION OF AGGRESSION

Aggression is defined as "an unprovoked attack or invasion," a derivative of the verb 'aggress,' which may be traced to its Latin base: ad-, to, and gradus, a step - to start a quarrel or to attack. The aggressor, then, is one who initiates attack upon another. The implications are those of impingement upon one's person, property, or holdings; of this being an active encroachment involving movement at least on the part of the initiator; and an inference of lack of provocation on the part of the aggrieved. This, then, is the classical definition. It may be refined to include <u>constructive</u> aggression: self-protective and preservative, realistically evoked by actual threat or danger, and should include healthful self-assertiveness necessary to protect one's own reasonable rights. Its counterpart is <u>destructive</u> aggression, not realistically essential for self-preservation or protection. The latter may be further subdivided: destructive behavior directed outward toward the environment, or toward persons or objects within it; or destructive behavior turned inward toward the self.

Ethology considers aggression to be an inherent, necessary, motivational force, a source of energy to be utilized for the enhancement of both the individual and the collective society, and hence a positive force; only maladaptive use of its energy, or improper defenses against it, bear a negative connotation. Over time the term 'aggression' has acquired a range of subjective, negative meanings, some of them averse to the ethological definition; these interpretations actually apply to the maladaptive direction of a vital and potentially constructive force.

In early evolutionary history there was no need for concern over human aggression. It served a basic function in man's direct struggle for food. But as civilization evolved and bonding patterns were established, instinctual forces were necessarily harnessed. It was here, perhaps, that man's problem in handling his aggressive forces first arose. For a price was affixed to this recantation of instinctual energy: defenses and repressors had to be established. Freud has astutely described the natural antagonism between the demands of instinct and the restrictions of civilization (4); certainly each of us is aware of the dilemma it can pose.

BRAIN MECHANISMS

Excitatory

The difficulty may lie, at least partially, in an adaptational lag in man's cerebral structure. The limbic system is the oldest segment of the cerebrum, which developed about 400 million years ago and reached its present peak of development 150 million years ago. It is here, in the limbic structure, that the <u>excitatory</u> potential for aggression exists -- in the deepest, most primitive portion of the brain, the hypothalamus, located in the brain stem. Feelings of anger originate here and are converted to neural-hormonal impulses with accompanying physiological changes -- rise in blood pressure, rapid heart beat, heavy breathing.

Inhibitory

But a rebus appears, for the <u>inhibitory</u> center, which controls anger and aggressive behavior, is located in the "large brain," the cerebral cortex. Its structures and functions in turn are modified and influenced by the "new brain," the neocortex. When feelings of anger, threat, or aggression arise, a series of inhibitory and related physiological changes occur. The body, while ready for action, is delayed or short-circuited in carrying out the action. Consequently, the "calming down" process is prolonged, for the physiological adjustments are in opposition to the original message. In view of the location of these initiating and controlling mechanisms, then, there appears to be a lapse, contributing to an inherent weakness, in the ability to handle human aggression. Predatory animals have evolved instinctual controls to avoid destruction of their own species members; and prey animals are equipped to flee, thus having no need for such controls. However, man has no strictly regulated mechanisms to deal with his aggressive impulses. He is relatively "unarmed" in terms of natural inhibitory endowment. Learned social controls are his major inhibitors, and they vary widely among societies and cultures. Regulatory rules, laws, religious and ethical standards sometimes impose harsh constraints upon the discharge of aggression.

BONDING

Yet we are social beings who need contact and communication
with others. Homo sapiens is totally unequipped to exist individually;
he needs and requires a society. Aggression rather paradoxically
facilitates our social organization. Early discovery of the benefits
to be derived from organizing into groups led to bond formation,
"behavior patterns of an objectively demonstrable mutual attachment
[which] constitute [a] personal tie." (9) In order to channel the original
energy of aggression into appropriate discharge and thus enhance human relationships, it must be redirected and canalized, for the bene-
fit of the group and for the individuals comprising the group.

Purpose

Thus bonds of friendship, love, common interests, or business
affiliations serve to redirect aggression into sublimated channels.
It is significant that bond behaviors are found only in those species
which are notably aggressive. Lorenz has cited numerous examples
of lower animal species in which bonding mechanisms do not exist;
they are characterized by loosely organized aggregations, one member readily exchanged for another, relationships being completely
impersonal (9). There is a wide range of human individual and group
behaviors serving this bonding function, from ritual food-sharing to
the familiar handshake, from the pomp and ceremony of an academic
procession to the observance of religious holidays. Cohesion and
stability, two factors necessary for the maintenance of a stable
group, are thus facilitated by bonding patterns of social interaction -- through the redirection of aggressive energy.

Role of Displacement

Tinbergen, in his detailed animal ethology studies, termed a
class of redirected behaviors displacement activities (11). When an
individual is caught up in a conflict of motives as, for example,
wanting to hit someone who has made him angry but simultaneously
restrained by training and inhibition, he may kick a chair or pound a
table. Scratching oneself may represent a displacement of inhibited
anger turned upon the self. It is thus a displacement activity derived from an intention movement but separated from the original
movement into a related behavior pattern. In this manner behavior
has undergone a change in function. While these displacement

activities do not necessarily serve a primary bonding function, they do provide a functional outlet for the discharge of aggression.

Suppressors and Consummatory Behaviors

We may add a second category of signal behaviors to the previously noted releaser group (Chapter 2) arising when biochemical energy demands release. This second group is comprised of suppressors, serving to redirect energy, deflecting it from its original intent into substitute channels. Repeated performance of a displacement activity leads to its becoming ritualized into a distinct new motor pattern. Many of the original patterns become compressed over time into simpler stereotyped form, facilitating their recognition and clarifying their signal function. These simplified patterns have been termed consummatory behaviors (3). We evidence a wide spectrum of these behaviors in our communicational anlage, particularly in the nonverbal realm of behavior.

RITUALIZATION

A key concept in the description of consummatory behaviors is that of ritualization. Ritualized behavior units have evolved from earlier fixed-action patterns, but some portions have become exaggerated in amplitude and frequency; they have also become simplified due to the dropping of some of their original components. Hinde notes that the "eyebrow lift of surprise" may well have evolved from an earlier "attention" signal (6). It has become ritualized and compressed into a simpler, readily recognized expression which we use in a variety of situations -- greeting, flirting, thanking, approving, questioning, emphasizing. This is a culturally determined ritualization, however, for some cultures have suppressed its performance; the Japanese, for example, consider the eyebrow lift indecent. "Coy behavior" -- downcast eyes, partial turning of the face and head -- is particularly evident among young girls of some cultures and seems to relate to an earlier "hiding" behavior, a ritualized ambivalence between approach and avoidance. Handshaking evolved as a means of demonstrating that no weapon was concealed in the right hand, while the word 'sinister' comes from the Latin 'sinister,' for left, indicating a crafty, sly person who would conceal a weapon in his left hand. The practice of raising one's hands in surrender has been ritualized into a behavior pattern implying "I don't know" or "I give up" when confronted with a puzzling or frustrating situation.

Ritualized movements often "freeze" over time into postures, establishing an adaptation at a higher level of integration. The erect stance of a male with legs apart, feet firmly planted, arms crossed over the chest seems to relate to an earlier sentinel posture; it is a "vigilance stance." Ritualized postures also serve the communicational process for they are readily understood, visible behaviors, which reduce ambiguity and thus enhance their signal function.

We should note, at this point, a differentiation between instinctive and cultural ritualization in the human species. Instinctive ritualized patterns, although influenced by the cultural group, occur in the linguistic-kinesic behavioral range and serve a positive communicatory function in the clarification of signals and response to them. Cultural ritualization has led to the development of specific rites, conventions, social norms and values. Both types of ritualization share the common attribute of familiarity and, hence, facile recognition. Of added significance is the frequency of rhythmic repetition -- in familiar ritualized behavior patterns and in rites, chants, and other culturally-evolved, ritualized ceremonies.

DOMINANCE

Huxley has noted that ritualization also assists in the reduction of conflict among group members (8). By virtue of man's abstracting abilities, words such as 'conflict' and 'attack' carry a range of meanings from overt physical assault to verbal insults and related symbolic inferences. There is another level of meaning, too -- that of establishing dominance or superiority over another or others. The term dominance, like aggression, has sometimes taken on a negative quality, blurring its original meaning. Dominance and submission characterize all societies, all relationships; dominance shifts, but it is an integral part of existence. Ethology relates dominance-submission to hierarchies of high to low rank. The pecking order of hens has been anthropomorphized in recent years to describe a host of social structures, and there are some striking analogies. Alpha may peck beta, beta cannot peck alpha but may peck gamma, etc. So John may not criticize his boss, whose decision he resents, but he may chastise his next subordinate, upon whom he vents his anger. Lorenz notes that tension is particularly high between individuals who hold immediately adjoining positions in the ranking order: tension lessens as distance in rank increases (9, page 45). Along similar lines Wynne-Edwards has defined society

as a "brotherhood of tempered rivalry" (13) -- tempered consider-
ably by ritualized behaviors.

Dominance is worked out in countless ways, in countless set-
tings, influenced by variables such as class, status, the issue, the
context. It is a necessary factor in any culture, but it seems a
troublesome one in contemporary America. Submission is difficult
for Americans to accept and so it is often denied, projected, dis-
torted, or otherwise turned to dysfunctional means. Among lower
animals "ritualized tests of strength" serve to establish dominance,
the weaker animal performing some gesture of submission in combination with the presentation of an especially vulnerable part of the
anatomy to the stronger animal. The dominant animal then permits
the submissive one to leave without having inflicted serious injury.
It is a sad commentary on our species that we often fail to perceive
such submissive messages. In fact, as Storr notes, "... it seems
that, for man, there is something about weakness or defeat which
actually increases hostility" (10).

Threat Behaviors

Dominance is often acquired by the performance of some kind of
threat behavior; these units are particularly evident in nonverbal behaviors although not necessarily accompanied by a verbal content of
threat or dominance. Nonverbal threat behavior may be effected by
posture, even by the foot. Particular elements of the face -- the
eyes, mouth, and teeth, for example -- are often used to display
threat. Eye contact and the length of gaze is also significant; an
overlong gaze becomes a stare and is generally considered hostile.
"Breaking gaze" may be construed as a submissive or avoidance
mechanism. Looking behavior is complex and cannot be interpreted
out of context; the situation and the participants determine the
meaning. Here, once again, symbolic processes must be considered -- the meaning attached to looking behavior, and being looked
at, may carry significant associations condensed from past experience related to dominance-submission, threat and appeasement.

Van Hooff notes the "tensed eye posture," eyes focused intently
in combination with the head slightly lowered and thrust forward, and
a slightly hunched posture (7). This is also known as the "mean
look" and conveys a definite threat signal. The kinesic movements
of threat behavior are closely related to those used in actual fighting,
often clearly derived from intention attack movements. These are

offensive threat behaviors. If, however, one is slightly unsure of himself or he is on the defensive, there may be a combination of attack and withdrawal behavior -- a clenched fist coupled with a backward stance, for example. An offensive threat movement will show marked attack components; a defensive threat will carry retreat signals.

We may briefly reconsider threat as it was noted in the context of the mother-child interaction. There threat is associated with the accumulation of tension and a state of unpleasure when some physical need of the infant is not met. It causes an increase in activity -- crying and motor movement. Conversely, a state of pleasure and satisfaction occurs when these needs are gratified; the infant becomes passive as he experiences contentment. So a state of gratification of needs becomes equated with pleasure and passivity, while unpleasure relates to threat and activity. But we cannot always maintain a state of nirvana, of oceanic contentment; so long as we live we will have to deal with threat in its many forms. Just as a certain degree of frustration is implicit in the process of learning and, indeed, may even enhance it, so threat is a fiber of the very process of living. How we perceive it and deal with it are the significant factors.

Submissive Behaviors

A class of ritualized behavior patterns which serve to inhibit aggression among group members has been termed submissive or appeasing behaviors. Lorenz favors the latter term, appeasing, because of its less subjective connotation. Many of these behaviors have evolved via selection pressure as an avoidance mechanism -- to prevent the stimulation of aggression in another. Numerous nonverbal expressive movements are behaviors of "social submissiveness," to facilitate friendly relations and adaptive communication. The appeasement grin (Fig. 2), with lower lip drawn down, sometimes exposing the teeth and gums, probably finds its origin in the primal expression of anxiety or fear; it is, in fact, also known as the "fear grin." This, in combination with an inhibited tendency to flee, has become ritualized into an appeasement expression. There are also appeasement postures, communicating fear in some instances, but also a frequent indicator of respect. A young adult male, applying for a job or conversing with an older, established male, is not likely to assume a dominant stance or seated "open" position. Yet among his peers he may do so. Role and status often determine the point, position, and presentation (Chapter 1) of the participants.

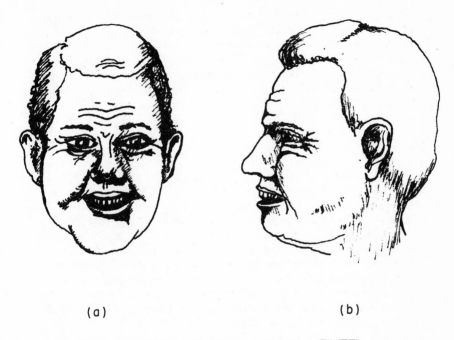

(a)   (b)

Figure 2. A friendly grin; an appeasement grin. Note the difference
in kinemes of the eye and mouth areas.

Appeasement behaviors are often the foundation of evolved social behaviors. So we permit another to enter a door before us, bow
deferentially to another, or approach an authority figure with an at-
titude of respect. These ritualized behaviors, often performed perfunctorily, are enormously important in the maintenance of a stable
social organization. There have been recent criticisms of this class
of behaviors; they have been deemed "empty rituals." And perhaps
some of them may yield to changing role, status, and class concepts.
But other behaviors of this class, appropriate to the times, must be
maintained in the service of communal stability and cohesion.

TERRITORY

The concept of territory is closely related to aggression. In
animal ethology, territorial behavior relates to geographical space;
Ardrey (1) defines it as "an area of space, whether land, sea or air,
which an animal defends as an exclusive preserve." Man, too, is a

territorial creature and similarly defends his property against pre-
dation, but human territorial imperative extends to a vast range of
constructs because of our ability to symbolize. We encounter territorial behavior daily; we react when our territory, whether a project, job, idea, social role, even a parking space, is usurped or
threatened. The greater our investment in any of these "areas,"
the more zealously we will guard it and resent the intrusion of others
on what we consider our "turf. "   .

Paranoid Hostility

We also react when we perceive our territorial rights threatened. Storr considers this factor to be man's greatest obstacle to
healthy utilization of aggression; he terms it "paranoid hostility"
(10, page 101). For despite our quite remarkable attributes and
abilities we do not always use them wisely. When the perception of
encroachment occurs, objectivity yields to subjectivity, distrust,
suspicion. Such a reaction often harkens back to our past, for we
react to present situations in terms of past experiences, condensed
by time and memory to present percepts. Or stresses may accumu-
late, distorting our perceptions. Or we may harbor negative, ir-
rational feelings toward ourselves but thrust them out, projecting
them onto another, or others, in vicious, hurting ways. Sometimes
we persuade others to join in our paranoid hostility and scapegoating
occurs, to the point of total extrusion from the group. These pro-
jections are often linked to some aspect of territorial rights or to
perceived threat of those rights.

Inciting Behaviors

Ethology defines the guardianship associated with territory as inciting behavior. We may "mark" our territory by verbally or kinesically defining it. Women are often skilled at marking
their marital or pair territory when another female exceeds its
boundaries; "He's mine" may be conveyed in many ways. A man ex-
presses turf rights when he says "This is my project, I started it
from scratch, and no advisory board is going to tell me how to run
it!" Or he may not verbalize it, but seek to undermine every plan
suggested or implemented by the advisory board. Inciting behavior
also includes those actions performed or messages conveyed which
set others to disagreeing, fighting, arguing. In this case it is a dis-
ruptive, bond-prohibiting mechanism. Strangely, in those instances,
the "incitor" does not seem to instigate consciously and is often not

aware of the role he plays. Inciting behaviors and territorial marking may often be seen in the realm of nonverbal communication as
well as in verbalized behavior.

SPACE

Intricately related to the concept of territory is the notion of
space. Its utilization and its meaning vary among cultures and, to
some extent, among individuals within these cultures. Ethnic groups
and nations living in crowded conditions necessarily share a higher
sensory involvement than those with more available space. So violation of space boundaries will relate, culturally, to the degree of
sensory stimulation serving as the norm. The concept of space and
spatial distancing is often a crucial factor in our ability in, or difficulty with, relating to others; yet we often fail to consider it in our
perception of others.

The concept of personal space is particularly relevant to the subject of nonverbal behaviors. Violation of one's personal space
boundaries may elicit a variety of protesting nonverbal responses --
from shifting to a closed and folded-in posture, to turning away from
the violator, to actually moving to another location when that is possible. Such violation of personal space boundaries seems to be dimly
perceived as threat, and some adaptation will inevitably ensue. If
the situation continues with no avenue of escape or sufficient adaptation possible, a state of anxiety with accompanying physiological
changes will occur.

Yet spatial perception includes other factors. von Uexkull describes three interpenetrating spatial areas "which complement, and
yet partially contradict, one another." Operational space refers to
the motor sphere of physical motion; tactile space is termed the
"locus sphere"; and visual space pertains to the circumscribed area
of vision at any point in time. These spatially defined areas thus
shift and change as the individual moves about.

Calhoun's studies of the effects of overcrowding on rat popula-
tions carry broad implications for spacing and space arrangements in
human groups. A pertinent finding was the direct correlation of
social dominance with territorial aggressiveness; the dominant males
established and maintained their territories successfully. Another
observation pertained to the development of pathological behavior
when overcrowding occurred, leading to emotional stress which, in
turn, triggered physiological changes. The final stage of disorder

was termed a "behavioral sink," in which all phases of individual and group behavior became grossly deteriorated (2, page 164). An interesting but less publicized finding pertains to Nb (the optimum or basic number for a species); it approximates twelve adult individuals for most orders of mammals, including the primates. Calhoun (2) observes that "Data from culturally primitive people strongly suggest that man emerged through such a lineage. I strongly suspect that man still bears the yoke or wears the diadem of an Nb-12."

Hall's studies of the cultural concepts of space, which he has termed Proxemics, led to his formulating four distancing zones for North Americans:

1. Zero to 1 1/2 ft for intimate relationships.
2. 1 1/2 ft to 4 ft for personal relationships.
3. 4 ft to 10 ft for social consultative relationships.
4. 10 ft and over for public interaction (5).

Simple observation can validate these findings as, for example, the space between a dating couple, mother and daughter when shopping, employee and supervisor in quick conference, and several persons waiting at a bus stop. Distancing zones do vary!

We have perhaps followed a circuitous path in our consideration of human aggression. But it is a necessarily involved route for this eidolon -- Aggression -- is both complex and dynamic. It is a potent factor in nonverbal behaviors as they interrelate with all levels of the communicational process. There is no neat, concise format for cataloging behaviors of this class. However, it is quite possible to become more aware of their range, of their potentials for both constructive and maladaptive use, and their intricate role in communication.

REFERENCES

1. Robert Ardrey. The Territorial Imperative. New York: Atheneum, 1966, p. 3.

2. John B. Calhoun, in Mental Health Program Reports-5. DHEW Publications, NIMH, 1971, p. 159.

3. W. Craig, "Appetites and aversions as constituents of instincts," Biol. Bull., 34, 91-107, 1918.

4. Sigmund Freud. Civilization and its Discontents (James Strachey, trans. and ed.). New York: W. W. Norton, 1961.

5. Edward Hall. The Hidden Dimension. New York: Doubleday & Co., 1966.

6. R. A. Hinde, (ed). Nonverbal Communication, Cambridge: The University Press, 1972.

7. J. A. R. A. M. van Hooff, in Primate Ethology (Desmond Morris, ed). New York: Doubleday (Anchor), 1969, p. 74.

8. Sir Julian Huxley. Ritualization of Behavior. Philosophical Transactions of the Royal Society of London, Series B, Vol. 251. London: The Royal Society, 1966.

9. Konrad Lorenz. On Aggression. New York: Harcourt Brace & World, 1966, p. 165.

10. Anthony Storr. Human Aggression. London: Atheneum Press, 1968. Bantam ed., p. 102.

11. Niko Tinbergen. The Study of Instinct. Oxford: The Clarendon Press, 1969 reprint.

12. Jakob von Uexkull cited in Instinctive Behavior (Claire Schiller, ed.). New York: International Univ. Press, 1957, p. 14.

13. V. C. Wynne-Edwards. Animal Dispersion in Relation to Social Behavior. Edinburgh: Oliver & Boyd, 1962.

FIVE

SOCIO-SEXUAL NONVERBAL BEHAVIORS

INTRODUCTION

If 'aggression' often carries a negative label in American culture, 'sex' seems to convey a positive stamp of approval. The present proliferation of sex education material attests to its popularity and acceptance, indicating perhaps a "naughty but nice" appeal. Yet sex and aggression cannot be considered as separate entities; they are closely, inextricably correlated in the filigree of human behavior. Kinsey notes that 14 physiological changes are common to both sexual and aggressive arousal, while only four such changes differ. He proposes a tentative hypothesis that if certain physiological elements were delayed or removed from developing into a sexual response, the resultant state might well become one of anger or fear (12).

Rather than labeling, let us consider sex as we did aggression -- a positive, vital force, with only its maladaptive canalization in such forms as rape, sadism, or violence carrying a minus sign. Because sexual behaviors in their derived forms involve interaction with others, they encompass the realm of social behaviors, too -- what is approved, what is taboo -- boundaries to define the range of acceptable conduct. Thus they often appear in combined form as socio-sexual behaviors. And the bonding implicit in their maintenance indicates a deflection of aggressive energy. There are positive selective advantages, too, in this range of socio-sexual behaviors, for they are simply incompatible with the expression of overt aggression.

Primary Sexual Behaviors

Primary sexual characteristics, the production of ova in the female and spermatazoa in the male, and the primary behaviors effecting their union, will be left to Dr. Reuben. However, a few general points should be noted as a background to the understanding of derived sexual behaviors. Humans are the only mammals capable of a face-to-face coital position, probably assumed following the evolution of an erect posture. It is a significant factor in primary sexual behavior, for it permits more interpersonal exchange between the partners.

Moreover, the human female does not experience periods of estrus or related fluctuating anatomic changes as do most classes of primates. Instead, there is a regular menstrual cycle and a constant

state of sexual receptivity. Thus there appears to be a greater need
for adaptational behaviors in the socio-sexual class. It may well explain, in conjunction with language skill and the ability to conceptualize, modification of originally sexual behaviors into the range of
combined socio-sexual behaviors among humans. Spitz has suggested that elements of human sexual behavior not only play an important role in personality formation but also serve extrasensory functions (16). So these activities, displays, and gestures, if placed in
the moral taboo category of primary sexual behaviors, could not be
used in the maintenance of social relations. However, when performed in combination with social grouping motivational behaviors,
they serve a combined function.

Evolutionary Changes in Hand, Face, and Brain

Biological changes in the brain, hand, and face are believed to
have followed the developed use of tools by early man. Selection
pressures continued their evolvement into highly specialized body
parts. Cerebral development in the frontal lobes, combined with the
manner in which the projection areas are connected with association
areas (particularly in the temporal lobes) provides for our ability to
conceptualize and verbalize. The human hand is also highly developed. Differential action between the two sides of the hand is
unique to man. There is a greater degree of motion between the ra-
dius and the first row of carpal bones than found in other primates.
The human thumb shows the greatest specialization in size, opposition, and strength (7).

The human face also shows a high degree of specialization for
expressive behavior; it has been estimated that over 20,000 facial
expressions are somatically possible. Van Hooff (10) notes "the
development of a facial musculature which eventually could become
the 'organ' of facial expression, apparently correlated with specialization of the sense of vision." Frijda's research on human facial expression suggests that selection has determined the eyes and the region around the eyes as a highly expressive area (9). It has been proposed that the development of a white region about the iris is an adaptation to accentuate the expressivity of the eyes (10, page 74). And
the cosmetics industry flourishes as women further highlight these
signal areas of the face!

Andrew has suggested that man's use of tears may well have
selective advantage, serving as displays which evoke defense and

assistance (1). Compound facial expressions are possible, with one expressive element directly influencing another. Certain facial postures may determine the quality of vocal presentation as, for example, when the lips and jaws are tightly compressed. So while the entire body is capable of expressive behavior, these highly specialized parts may express a gamut of subtle discriminations in the nonverbal repertoire.

Yet, despite their complexity and the large number of expressions, gestures, and postures possible, each culture selects a small number which become traditionalized by its members. This selection process simplifies and clarifies communication for group members. It is also intricately related to their speech behavior and cognitive-perceptual schema. To date American kinesic research has revealed that, of the large number of possible expressive behaviors, Americans use only about 30 gestures and perhaps 25 postural configurations. They are used repetitively, each individual having his unique style, but within the acceptable and easily recognized range of his cultural group.

Visual Interaction

Visual interaction is an integral part of social behavior. It may be a one-way glance, a dyadic mutual glance, or an encompassing sweep of the group. Glances vary from one to seven seconds, whereas visual scanning consists of sweeps of .25 to .35 seconds in duration. Argyle notes that Americans engaged in conversation will look at each other from 30% to 60% of the time; there will be intermittent mutual glances mixed with one-way glances. American women look at their partner in conversation to a greater extent than do men, particularly when talking to other women (3). Kendon has found that Americans usually look up just prior to the completion of an utterance, or at the moment of completion, probably seeking nonverbal reaction to their remarks (11). He also notes that absence of this terminal look results in an overly long pause before the other replies; it is so much a part of the American nonverbal level that its absence upsets the communicational rhythm. We look away as we begin to speak, usually, in order to mentally organize our comments and to avoid distraction.

Smiles and Laughter

Smiles and laughter often accompany socio-sexual behaviors.
The many types and gradients of smiles have not yet been thoroughly
researched; the number somatically possible is great, and cultural
situations eliciting a smiling response vary. It does seem certain
that smiling and laughter represent different intensities of the same
behavior pattern and, in fact, often alternate with each other.
Laughing may have served originally as an appeasement or greeting
ceremony, smiling having evolved later at a lower threshold of excitation (13). Both may of course be feigned in social situations,
giving rise to the term "reception smile," but these contrived responses are usually perceived as false. Van Hooff notes the bonding
quality of shared laughter when a joke is told among friends; he refers to it as "intellectual social play" (10, page 76). Sometimes a
smile may serve as a meta-communication, i.e., a message about
how a communication is to be taken (4)-- "I'm only joking," for example.

PAIR BOND

Nurturing: Symbolism

The norm for sexual behavior in both its basic and derived form
is that of a dyad, or pair. Pair formation is necessary to any kind
of social organization, and some kind of bonding device is necessary
for its realization. In its most basic form the pair bond provides for
reproduction, brood care, and nourishment -- "nesting behaviors."
While the derived levels of pair behavior may not be so basically
oriented, they do retain some aspect of the nurturing function. The
very concept of pair, and also group, behavior bespeaks a need for
relatedness and nurturance. When the nurturing is reciprocal,
bonding is mutually enhanced. Among humans nurturing takes many
forms, appears in many guises, occurs in countless situations. But
it signifies a symbolic feeding, a response to some need or a recognition of some signaled need. While these signals may not be verbalized or overtly acknowledged, they do occur and frequently occur
in the kinesic range of behaviors. Ardrey's comment, "The pair is
a social arrangement with sexual convenience of varying reward,"
(2) may certainly be applied to human pair behavior in both its instinctual and symbolic processes.

Postural Configurations

There are two postural configurations assumed in pair behavior (14). The vis-a-vis position (Fig. 3) refers to two persons
facing each other as they interact -- the student with his faculty ad-
viser, an employee with his supervisor, two friends in conversation.
There is frequent eye contact and a reciprocal linguistic-kinesic exchange between them. A pair may, however, be oriented toward a
third person or an object -- a movie screen, for example -- yet evidence rapport in their shared postures. These are parallel postures
and the postural orientations are complementary to each other (Fig.
4). The two may assume a "mirror" posture of one another; this is
termed mirror-image. Or they may share direct, identical postural
configurations. Both mirror-image and direct dyadic postural relationships are considered congruent; they occur in both vis-a-vis and
parallel body orientations. Both configurations may be observed
within larger group contexts and usually indicate an alignment or
some shared advocacy or rapport between the two persons.

SECONDARY SEXUAL BEHAVIORS

Gender Displays

Nonverbal sexual behaviors relate to secondary sexual characteristics (the anatomical differences) and to tertiary (or learned)
culturally-determined features. Ethologists would refer to these
behaviors as "gender displays." They serve to (1) signal gender;
(2) provide a response to an initial gender signal; and (3) establish
or heighten interest, maintain rapport, and generally enhance relatedness in social situations. They may also serve as a bonding
mechanism between individuals, varying in duration from a few seconds to the entire course of a relationship.

There are some noticeable differences in male and female gender display. Birdwhistell has noted two postural examples. American females, in sending or responding to male signals, bring the
legs together while the male position is one in which the intrafemoral
index is a 10- to 15-degree angle. In use of the arm, the female
holds her upper arm close to the trunk, while the male moves his
arm five to ten degrees away from the body (6). Ethnic and regional
variables may influence to what degree these differences will de displayed and to what extent they will be amplified or compressed.

Figure 3. Vis-a-vis postural configuration, a reciprocal position.

Figure 4. Parallel postural orientation. The two figures on the left share complementary postures.

Leg and Foot Positions

Leg and foot positions in sitting postures also differ. American females may sit with their legs crossed at the knees; the ankles may be crossed or the legs intertwined; feet may be placed on the floor, sometimes with one foot extended further. In some situations it is permissible for a female to fold one or both legs under her in a sitting posture; this seems to define the situation as either (a) informal or (b) contemplative. Mode of dress may influence leg position and posture to some degree.

American males may cross their legs at or above the knee, but often sit with legs apart and feet planted on the floor. The broken-four position consists of an ankle positioned on the other knee. This leg position indicates some degree of informality; it is often observed among males of higher rank or status in a group situation. At times a male may shift into the broken-four position to effect a modified barrier to an opinion or another person.

DERIVED SOCIO-SEXUAL BEHAVIORS

The derived socio-sexual behaviors may be subdivided into two groups: individual, self-orienting activities, and communicational, other-directed behaviors. We are, of course, more concerned with the latter because of their interpersonal nature. But we should become familiar with the former in order to recognize and distinguish them from the communicational behaviors. However, it should also be noted that they often occur "in mix," individual behaviors being performed while communicational activities are simultaneously occurring.

Individual

Individual socio-sexual behaviors are also known as auto-grooming or preening; they relate to care of the body surface, are ministrations or services to the self. Women tend to touch their hair, particularly at the sides of the head or at the nape of the neck; tuck in a blouse, check their make-up. The male may straighten or stroke his tie, brush his hand over his trouser leg, stroke his moustache, or rub his chin. Foot jiggling and fingernail inspection occur in both sexes. Not all of these behaviors hold particular meaning: they may be an instance of simple motor discharge of tension. Sometimes they serve as displacement activities directed

toward the self. Their specific meaning cannot be determined un-
less the context and the ongoing behavioral sequence are known.

Communicational

Communicational behaviors in the socio-sexual range fall into
two main categories: (1) invitational, or permissive; and (2) prohibiting, or rejecting behaviors. They will be performed within the
range of the individual's particular body set but will vary within that
range depending upon the interactional sequence. And they, too,
occur "in mix," for each of us uses both permissive and rejecting
expressive behaviors.

A female invitational posture frequently observed is the breast
presentation -- arms drawn toward the back of the torso, or one or
both arms draped over the back of a chair, or arms raised over the
head so that the breast is protruded, "displayed." Eric Berne has
termed this posture "advertising," either ethically, e.g., with
pride, or subversively, or even competitively with exploitation the
intent (5). A shift into or out of this posture will usually be accompanied by a related shift in the verbal exchange and the affective
quality accompanying it.

Presentation of the wrist and palm is a reliable gestural indicator of female invitational behavior. Of course, palm presentation
occurs in many contexts and is performed by both sexes. But when
it includes presentation of the wrist, too, and is performed by a female during a social exchange, it may be assumed to represent an
invitational, attracting gesture. It need not indicate overt sexual receptivity, however; it is rather a "qualified" nonverbal behavior.

A typical male invitational posture consists of a pronounced
forward lean, particularly of the upper torso, with a pulling-in of
the abdominal muscles and squaring of the shoulders. There is
frequent eye contact with the female, and a slight sideways glance is
sometimes used. Hand gestures are often alternately directed
toward himself and toward the female.

Prohibiting behaviors are found at all levels of nonverbal communication. They include postures, gestures, and markers, all of
which may (but not necessarily) relate to the verbal content. Arms
folded across the chest (Fig. 5) may signal distancing or subdued
involvement in an interaction; it may indicate disagreement with a

Figure 5. Barrier behavior. The crossed arms and facial expression signal a qualified distancing or blocking intent, not always consciously performed.

comment or viewpoint expressed by another. We easily recognize the rejecting gesture of one or both arms extended with palms turned out. Frowning may indicate disapproval or disagreement, although it also accompanies deep concentration. Posture and stance may indicate withdrawal or distaste, particularly when a postural shift occurs -- a pulling back or drawing away from a person or idea or from an emotion associated with a topic. Barrier behavior may be effected by positioning oneself between two persons, and in more subtle ways -- a leg extended, hand and arm sweeps, interfering gestures. Violation of personal space boundaries will elicit some form of "blocking" or barrier behavior -- pulling the upper torso back, crossed arms, crossed legs. An individual may not display gender signals appropriate to his or her sex; their omission may signify an unconscious <u>self</u>-prohibition of socio-sexual adaptation.

Figure 6. Bookending. The two end figures lean in toward the others and share mirror-image postures.

Postural Configurations

We have previously noted the pattern and order of systems, languages, and cultures and of individual kinesic "body-set" behavior. There is also pattern and order in postural relationships within groups, patterns of repetitive behaviors among the group members. They are highly interdependent, serving a regulatory function both for the individuals and for group stability. As we interact with others we also engage in a monitoring process -- cross-referencing subjective data with that of the ongoing behavioral sequence. It is thus rather easy to assess alignments and realignments at any point in time -- shared postures, subgroup formations, barrier behaviors; for postural configurations hold communicative meaning. As Scheflen notes, "Communication, then, includes all behaviors by which a group forms, sustains, mediates, corrects, and integrates its relationships" (14, page 318).

Mixed postural configurations also contribute to group process, accomplished by splitting the body congruence. So an individual may share an upper torso position with one group member, while his leg and foot position maintain complementarity with another. These mixed configurations are usually performed unconsciously, yet they contribute to group cohesion and relatedness. They may be considered as kinesic bonding mechanisms.

"Bookending" may be noted in a group when members are seated or standing in a row, the person at each end assuming a posture or stance inward toward the others (Fig. 6). This

configuration is often assumed along the side of a conference table
and at social events when several persons are positioned in a line.
It tends to confine those within the group and to limit its member-
ship (14, page 326).

Quasi-Courtship Behaviors

Scheflen has identified and described a class of derived socio-
sexual behaviors which he has termed "quasi-courtship" structures (15). Quasi-courting differs from actual courtship performance due to the inclusion of various "qualifiers" and "disclaimers." The qualifiers refer to kinesic behaviors -- incomplete postural units, nonverbal references to the context (arm sweeps, gestures to include others, etc.). Disclaimers occur at the lexical
level -- verbally noting the presence of others, mentioning the reason for their being together, joking.

Several basic elements occur in succession during performance
of these quasi-courtship units. Courtship readiness must first be
introduced, although the participants may not be aware that it occurs.
The torso becomes more erect; a sagging posture may be corrected;
muscle tonus increases, particularly in the legs; eyes may appear
brighter; interest seems generally heightened. At this point auto-
grooming (preening) by either or both the male and female may be
noted. Concurrent with, or closely following these signals, flirta-
tious behaviors occur -- smiles, change in voice inflection, increased eye contact. Some form of allogrooming may be performed -- brushing a speck of lint from the other's clothing, as-
sisting the other in some grooming activity; the male may light her
cigarette.

These behaviors continue until one or both of the pair de-court,
or withdraw, from the sequence. Scheflen provides five contexts in
which de-courting may occur: (1) when gender confusion cannot be
resolved, (2) when there is ambiguity about the situation due to con-
fusing qualifiers, (3) if one or the other quasi-courts too intensely,
(4) when the partner or the group in which this behavior occurs cannot tolerate its tension, and (5) when others actively interfere (as
with barrier behavior). These are not overt sexual behaviors but
modified, positive socio-sexual repertoires, serving to heighten
interest and sustain relatedness.

Greeting Behaviors

Greeting behaviors are also of the socio-sexual class. They include certain gestures, postures, vocal inflections unique to the
greeting rite. There is a quick eyebrow-lift of recognition, perhaps
some form of tactile contact -- handshake, hug, kiss, embrace --
culturally and situationally determined. Eibl-Eibesfeldt notes that in
addition to the 1/6-second eyebrow flash, members of many diverse
cultures also greet by raising the open hand (8). Greeting behaviors
serve a discriminatory function for two participants -- all others are
excluded. When one enters a room where others are present, some
form of greeting occurs -- eyebrow flash, head nod, eye sweep to include the group. This is the initial step in the interactional sequence. In ethological terms the greeting rite is an appeasement
ceremony, serving as a suppressor; it also functions as an efficient
releaser of action patterns in others due to its regularity of performance within the cultural range of the participants.

Parting Rites

There are also parting rites, performed perfunctorily, serving
as terminals to the interaction. Parting behaviors are often informal
but still possess a pattern of movement; spatial distancing increases
as one, both, or all participants move away from the meeting site.
Postures and gestures tend to be directed away from the group; the
head and eyes particularly convey termination in this manner. If a
group member prolongs the parting situation, individual behaviors
conveying impatience may be seen -- avoidance of eye contact,
turning the torso away from the malingerer, leaning back or step-
ping back, foot tapping, or rocking on the heels.

SUMMARY

All of these socio-sexual behaviors serve a necessary function in
the maintenance of positive social relations. An understanding of
their range and performance may enhance interaction with others.
Once again we should note the affinity of sex and aggression or, in
ethological terms, of agonistic and socio-sexual behaviors, in all of
the communicational modalities. In pair behavior, at a social gath-
ering or business meeting, even in a quick hallway conference between co-workers, one may see quasi-courting interspersed with
threat behavior, invitational gestures, and appeasement sequences,
prohibitory and permissive cues in the pageant of human behavior.

One is reminded of Eddington's marvelous aphorism: "We once thought that if we know 'one' we know 'two' because one and one equals two but we have since found we must learn a deal more about 'and'." So with sex and aggression, an enigma sometimes exists in the mystical 'and.'

REFERENCES

1. R. J. Andrew, "Evolution of facial expression," Science, 142, 1041 (1963).

2. Robert Ardrey. The Territorial Imperative. New York: Atheneum, 1966, p. 81.

3. Michael Argyle. The Psychology of Interpersonal Behavior. Middlesex: Penguin Books, 1967, p. 115.

4. Gregory Bateson, "The message: This is play," in Group Processes (B. Schaffner, ed.) Vol. 2. Madison, New Jersey: Madison Printing Co., 1955.

5. Eric Berne. Sex in Human Loving. New York: Simon & Schuster, 1970, pp. 68-69.

6. Ray L. Birdwhistell. Kinesics and Context. Philadelphia: University of Pennsylvania Press, 1971, p. 44.

7. Sterling Bunnell. Surgery of the Hand (3rd. ed.). Philadelphia: Lippincott, 1956, p. 26.

8. Iranaus Eibl-Eibesfeldt. Ethology: The Biology of Behavior. New York: Holt, Rinehart & Winston, 1970, p. 420.

9. N. H. Frijda as noted in Reference 10, p. 74.

10. J. A. R. A. M. van Hooff, in Primate Ethology (Desmond Morris, ed.), New York: Doubleday (Anchor) 1969, p. 80.

11. A. Kendon, "Some functions of gaze direction in social interaction," Acta Psychologica, 26, 22-63 (1967).

12. A. Kinsey, W. B. Pomeroy, C. E. Martin and P. Gebhard. Sexual Behavior in the Human Female. Philadelphia: Saunders & Co., 1953, p. 704.

13. Konrad Lorenz. On Aggression. New York: Harcourt Brace & World, 1966, p. 171.

14. A. E. Scheflen, "The significance of posture in communication systems," Psychiatry, 27, 326-327 (1964).

15. A. E. Scheflen, "Quasi-courtship behavior in psychotherapy," Psychiatry, 28, 245-257 (1965).

16. Rene Spitz, "Autoeroticism re-examined: The role of early sexual behavior patterns in personality formation," The Psychoanalytic Study of the Child, 17, 283-315 (1962).

EPILOGUE

Our perusal of the various modalities of human communication, with particular emphasis on the nonverbal behaviors, has shown us to be quite remarkable creatures. We have examined the nature of open systems, noting the vast potential offered by the new systems theory in understanding many and diverse phenomena. Within the framework of natural science we have recognized the pattern and order which prevail within a system, be it language, body motion, culture, or speech behavior. The pattern and order further yield evidence of a natural rhythmicity among the parts or sequences, oscillations of varying intensities, which contribute to the uniqueness of each entity.

We have examined the biologic base of kinesic behavior, the myriad variations in the learned repertoire, and the range of individual variations contributing to the diversity among people. We have pursued the role and significance of human aggression and the aggregate of agonistic behaviors -- dominance, threat, appeasement, territory, space -- and their related concepts. Among the motor patterns, both releasers and suppressors have been noted as functional modes of kinesic communication. The continuum from appetitive to consummatory behaviors demonstrates a wide range of expressive mechanisms. The socio-sexual behaviors comprise a class of positive bonding mechanisms in the service of social organization and cohesion.

To utilize these concepts it is not necessary to memorize the levels of speech behavior delineated by Sapir or the nomenclature employed in kinesics research. One does not need to list the properties of a fixed-action pattern as compared with a redirected intention movement. Far more relevant is an increased awareness of ourselves living within a universe of natural law, persons with tremendous capabilities of expression at many levels. Our language skills are both an asset and a liability; speech behavior serves as a primary mode of communication, yet we are so "locked in" to the verbal content that we fail to realize the rich array of expression in the kinesic range. We are often semi-aware of nonverbal expression in ourselves and in others; it is rather easy to enhance this "sensing" as we become attuned to its structure, function, and scope. Now,

perhaps more than at any time in human history, it is imperative
that we assess our place in the natural universe and strive to facilitate the human discourse.

The twentieth century has produced marvels of technology that
only the most imaginative could have foretold. Computer and electronic devices serve as extensions of human communication at the
speed of light. Digital technology can produce masses of data, figures, information, statistical analyses at the touch of a button.
There is an ever increasing tendency to think, and speak, in terms
of masses -- mass data, mass transit, mass media, mass communication. The cycle of change has been swift; tension, unrest, shifting values and ideologies attest to our distress and bewilderment.
Often a lurking fear is the loss of one's individuality, of becoming
merely a series of computerized card identities -- "Please do not
fold, spindle, or mutilate me!" Man, the creature of Nature, now
ponders this mass mechanization with ambivalence, weighing progress against fear.

The benefits to be derived from this technological explosion are
legion if we but remember that masses are composed of individuals.
The gradient is always there, from the vast ecosystem downward to
the individual or from molecule upward to organisms of great complexity. It exemplifies the paradox of the human condition -- the individual and yet of the species. To be freed of our own limitations
we must depend upon the skills, knowledge, and contributions of
others, upon the diversity of data processing and the widespread
dissemination of information. Yet the uniqueness of the individual
must be maintained in the service of human tradition.

This recognition of the individual -- a singular personality with
aspirations, needs, wishes, apprehensions -- may be further enhanced by increasing our awareness of the diversity among people,
cultures, nationalities. And this diversity extends to encompass
perceptions, language use, kinesics -- all of behavior. Symbolism
and the world of symbolic processes adds a dimension of significance for all humans everywhere. To deny differences among
people is to overlook the beauty to be found in variety. Communication is mutually enhanced through a recognition and response to individual variations. The increasing number of American minority
persons now entering colleges and universities points to this need;
foreign exchange students represent varied cultural backgrounds.
And beyond the academic concourse there is the larger community

and its inhabitants, often representing a variety of socio-economic groups.

It is not mere coincidence that 'community' and 'communication' are so similar; both share a Latin-derived base, which translates common, or shared. Over the course of human history we have shown proclivity to fragment into groups, each group having a particular set of morals, rites, traditions. While serving many positive functions, there has also been a Janus aspect; often a group, culture, or nation has then proceeded to establish dominance over others. By scorn, ridicule, and rejection these "others" have been branded inferior by the collectivity seeking dominance. In addition to the tragic consequences of war, hatred, and violence, those subjugated acquire a negative identity. At first defensive, then submissive, they harbor rage at the inequity, internalizing it where it becomes self-hate. The rage mounts until shifting social, economic, and political circumstances unite to provide a setting for the eruption of violence. If the human mind can conceive and implement countless mechanical marvels, creations of great beauty in all the modes of art, wonders from the world of science, surely it can leash these furies which beset us and turn them to positive bonding service. For we are all of one species: Man, who, by virtue of geographic and historic lineage, has evolved social and communicatory systems adapted to the group's particular circumstance in time and space.

The remaining years of the twentieth century signify a time of tremendous challenge. We stand at a crossroads. Will we continue the route of fragmentation and its inevitable consequences, hatred and violence? Or will we perhaps follow the path of gloom predicted by those who foresee gross human mechanization and alienation the inevitable outcome of the technological explosion? Or may we join in a celebration of human capabilities enhanced by human invention as we seek a sense and spirit of community?

For those in the media, library, and information professions, who have already pioneered new methods of transmittal and retrieval service, there is a new challenge -- the reinforcement of 'community' by way of 'communication.' Understanding variance in territorial perception, variance in differential space use, nonverbal cues of appeasement, postural indicators of rapport, the functions served by kinesic behaviors and the responses they elicit: all may heighten our awareness of this shared community of being we call human. Certainly it will not grant omniscience or a solution to all problems.

But it may provide a significant bonding mechanism at a crucial point in our history. Our study of nonverbal behavior and its role in the total communicational process has revealed a complexity not yet fully realized. We are truly remarkable beings -- contrary at times, troublesome and difficult, fearful and anxious, too -- but possessing great adaptive potential. Let us seek for community and approach the task with humility.

AUTHOR INDEX

Andrew, R. J., 63
Ardrey, Robt., 56, 65
Argyle, M., 64
Arlow, J. A., 40

Bacon, Francis, 2
Bateson, Gregory, 8, 65
Benedict, Ruth F., 6
Berne, Eric, 69
Bernstein, Basil, 42
Bertalanffy, L. von, 7, 43-44
Birdwhistell, R. L., 8, 9, 12, 39, 41, 66
Bloomfield, L., 6, 38
Boaz, F., 38
Bowlby, John, 26
Brierley, M., 28
Brosin, H. W., 8, 9
Bunge, Mario, 13
Bunnel, S., 63

Calhoun, John, 58
Cannon, W. B., 29
Cohen, Rosalie A., 42
Coleman, D. J., 27
Condon, W. S. 9, 40
Craig, W., 18, 21

D'Abro, A., 13
Darwin, Chas., 18, 23-25, 28
Descartes, R., 4
Dewey, John, 5

Efron, D., 41-42
Eibl-Eibesfeldt, I., 74
Estienne, Henri, 2

Freud, Sigmund, 19, 27, 48
Frijda, H. H., 63
Frisch, Otto von, 18
Fromm-Reichmann, F., 8

Goldstein, Kurt, 7

Hall, Edward T., 58
Harris, Z. S., 6
Hartmann, G. W., 6
Heinroth, Oscar, 18
Hinde, R. A., 18, 51
Hockett, Chas., 8
Hooff, J. A. R. A. M. von, 53, 63, 65
Huxley, Julian, 18, 20

James, William, 5, 28

Kendon, A., 64
Kinsey, A. C., 62

Loeb, F. F., 27
Lorenz, K., 12, 18, 22, 50, 52, 54

McQuown, N. A., 6, 8
Morris, D., 76
Murdoch, G. P., 35

SUBJECT INDEX

Other books
of interest
to you...

Because of your interest in our books, we have included the following catalog of books for your convenience.

Any of these books are available on an approval basis. This section has been reprinted in full from our **library science** catalog.

If you wish to receive a complete catalog of MDI books, journals and encyclopedias, please write to us and we will be happy to send you one.

MARCEL DEKKER, INC.
270 Madison Avenue, New York, N. Y. 10016

library science
information science
computer science

ARNETT and KENT *Computer Based Chemical Information*

(Books in Library and Information Science Series, Volume 4)

edited by EDWARD ARNETT, *Department of Chemistry, University of Pittsburgh, Pennsylvania,* and ALLEN KENT, *Director, Office of Communication Programs, University of Pittsburgh, Pennsylvania*

280 pages, illustrated. 1973

Concerned with the development of a variety of computer–searchable indexes. Describes experiences arising from a major experimental program in accessing some of these data bases in order to provide them to a large group of chemists, and includes behavioral studies on the use of the literature by chemists before and after the introduction of these services. A great aid to librarians, chemical information officers, research directors, and research chemists.

CONTENTS: The research chemist and his information environment, *E. Arnett and A. Kent.* The Pittsburgh Chemical Information Center—internal and external interactions, *E. Arnett and A. Kent.* The user's information system: An evaluative research approach, *D. Amick.* System design, implementation, and evaluation, *N. Grunstra and J. Johnson.* Interactive retrieval systems, *E. Caruso.* Chemistry library, *M. Roppolo.* Approaches to the economical retrospective machine-searching of the chemical literature, *B. El-Hadidy and D. Amick.*

BEKEY and SCHWARTZ
Hospital Information Systems

(Biomedical Engineering Series, Volume 1)

edited by GEORGE A. BEKEY, *University of Southern California, Los Angeles,* and MORTON D. SCHWARTZ, *California State College, Long Beach*

416 pages, illustrated. 1972

Brings together the current knowledge on hospital information systems, previously scattered in diverse publications involved in the implementation of hospital information systems. Among the main areas covered are: the clinical laboratory, the hospital ward, the intensive care unit, the coronary care unit, the pharmacy, the multi-test screening center, and the business office. Of vital interest to hospital administrators, biomedical engineers, medical computer research workers, architects, physicians, nurses, paramedical workers, and all others concerned with the modernization of medical care.

CONTENTS: Review of hospital information systems, *E. C. DeLand and B. W. Waxman.* Status of hospital information systems, *M. D. Schwartz.* Electronic data processing of prescriptions, *R. F. Maronde and S. Seibert.* On-line data bank for admissions, laboratories, and clinics, *G. E. Thompson.* Hospital information system effectiveness, *E. J. Bond.* Data processing techniques for multitest screening and hospital facilities, *M. F. Collen.* Automation and computerization of clinical laboratories, *M. D. Schwartz.* Computing systems in hospital laboratories, *M. J. Ball, J. C. Ball, and E. A. Magnier.* Computer applications in acute patient care, *M. D. Schwartz.* A computer-based information system for patient care, *H. R. Warner.* Use of automated techniques in the management of the critically ill, *M. H. Weil, H. Shubin, L. D. Cady, Jr., H. Carrington, N. Palley, and R. Martin.* Retrospect and overview, *G. A. Bekey.*

DAILY *The Anatomy of Censorship*

(Books in Library and Information Science Series, Volume 6)

by JAY E. DAILY, *Graduate School of Library and Information Sciences, University of Pittsburgh, Pennsylvania*

400 pages, illustrated. 1973

An analysis of the motives of the censor, rather than a history of censorship. Exposes the essential purposes of censorship: the maintenance of a propaganda line, the preservation of stereotypes, and the limitation of knowledge.

CONTENTS: Don't touch my dirty words • The horses of instruction • The tigers of wrath • The road of excess • The palace of wisdom • The awakened sex • Sensuous education • To turn a trick • Intellectual freedom and the world community.

DAILY *Organizing Nonprint Materials*

(Books in Library and Information Science Series, Volume 3)

by JAY E. DAILY, *Graduate School of Library and Information Sciences, University of Pittsburgh, Pennsylvania*

200 pages, illustrated. 1972

Presents the means for organizing collections of nonprint material so that the highest level of efficiency combines with the most effective service to the community. Provides a critical introduction to the understanding of both the problems and possibilities of organizing nonprint collections. Examines specialized tools used in organizing picture collections, and provides a list of uniform titles, a list of subject headings for phonorecordings, and other examples of cataloging nonprint material. Also includes an extensive bibliography to guide the reader to supplementary information.

CONTENTS: Nonprint materials, a problem of definition • Defining the library and its patrons • Pictures and other nonprint material that contains no self-description • Recorded sound • Motion pictures • The procedural manual for nonprint materials • Community survey • Community survey of the Media Center of the Graduate School of Library and Information Sciences of the University of Pittsburgh • Procedural manual • Sources for audiovisual materials • Cataloging phonorecordings • Exogenous description • Classified list of subject headings • Alphabetized list of subject headings.

MANHEIMER *Style Manual: A Guide for the preparation of Reports and Dissertations*

(Books in Library and Information Science Series, Volume 5)

by MARTHA L. MANHEIMER, *Graduate School of Library and Information Sciences, University of Pittsburgh, Pennsylvania*

200 pages, illustrated. 1973

Designed to resolve the problems of anyone working towards a degree and also of value to other students preparing dissertations and term papers who have found other style manuals inadequate. Provides models of bibliographic references for all types of material commonly referred to, and establishes patterns for internal format used to structure the content of the dissertation. Highly useful for any scholarly paper in the field of library and information science and related areas.

CONTENTS: Introduction • Quotations • Bibliographic references • Authorship or entry element • Corporate authorship and documents • Periodicals, other serials, and archives • Chapter references and the bibliography.

WILLIAMS, MANHEIMER, and DAILY
Classified Library of Congress Subject Headings

(Books in Library and Information Science Series, Volumes 1 and 2)

by JAMES WILLIAMS, MARTHA L. MANHEIMER, and JAY E. DAILY, *Graduate School of Library and Information Sciences, University of Pittsburgh, Pennsylvania*

Vol. 1 *Classified List*
296 pages, illustrated. 1972

Vol. 2 *Alphabetic List*
512 pages, illustrated. 1972

Provides, for the first time, a complete and consecutive listing of all Library of Congress suggested classification numbers along with their corresponding subject headings. Volume 1 contains a list of classification numbers in classified order, together with their subject headings (including subheadings and sub-subheadings) that appear in the 7th edition of the Library of Congress List. Volume 2 consists of an alphabetical listing of the classified subject headings contained in Volume 1, with their respective classification numbers. In this volume, unused or obsolete headings are cross referenced with the legal classified subject headings.

The reader can locate in the alphabetical listing the general category of the book to be cataloged, find this category in the classified list, and then easily choose its exact subject heading. Absolutely essential volumes for every cataloger, librarian, and library school. Also of value to researchers in any field who need to relate subject headings directly to classification numbers.

—————— OTHER BOOKS OF INTEREST ——————

MATTSON, MARK, and MacDONALD
Computer Fundamentals for Chemists

(Computers in Chemistry and Instrumentation Series, Volume 1)

edited by JAMES S. MATTSON, *Rosenstiel School of Marine and Atmospheric Sciences, University of Miami, Florida,* HARRY B. MARK, JR., *Department of Chemistry, University of Cincinnati, Ohio,* and HUBERT C. MACDONALD, JR., *Koppers Company, Inc., Monroeville, Pennsylvania*

384 pages, illustrated. 1973

MATTSON, MARK, and MacDONALD
Electrochemistry: Calculations, Simulation, and Instrumentation

(Computers in Chemistry and Instrumentation Series, Volume 2)

edited by JAMES S. MATTSON, *Rosenstiel School of Marine and Atmospheric Sciences, University of Miami, Florida,* HARRY B. MARK, JR., *University of Cincinnati, Ohio,* and HUBERT C. MACDONALD, JR., *Koppers Company, Inc., Monroeville, Pennsylvania*

488 pages, illustrated. 1972

MATTSON, MARK, and MacDONALD
Spectroscopy and Kinetics

(Computers in Chemistry and Instrumentation Series, Volume 3)

edited by JAMES S. MATTSON, *Rosenstiel School of Marine and Atmospheric Sciences, University of Miami, Florida,* HARRY B. MARK, JR., *Department of Chemistry, University of Cincinnati, Ohio,* and HUBERT C. MACDONALD, JR., *Koppers Company, Inc., Monroeville, Pennsylvania*

352 pages, illustrated. 1973

SACKS *Measurements and Instrumentation in the Chemical Laboratory*

by RICHARD D. SACKS, *Department of Chemistry, University of Michigan, Ann Arbor*

in preparation. 1973

SACKS and MARK *Simplified Circuit Analysis: Digital Analog Logic*

by RICHARD D. SACKS, *University of Michigan, Ann Arbor, and* HARRY B. MARK, JR., *University of Cincinnati, Ohio*

176 pages, illustrated. 1972

———————— ENCYCLOPEDIAS OF INTEREST ————————

ENCYCLOPEDIA OF COMPUTER SCIENCE AND TECHNOLOGY

edited by JACK BELZER, ALBERT G. HOLZMAN and ALLEN KENT, *University of Pittsburgh, Pennsylvania*

Subscription Price: $50.00 per volume

Single Volume Price: $60.00 per volume

in preparation. 1973

This *Encyclopedia* covers every aspect of computer technology and the fields in which computer technology is used. The scope is developed by the enumeration of an alphabetical list of topics ranging from the specific to the generic. It examines the history and development of computers, the current state of computer science, and the role computers will play in our society in the future. Treatment of subject matter is straightforward, yet scholarly and exhaustive, so that the articles are both comprehensible to the layman and stimulating to the informed specialist. The *Encyclopedia* is of utmost interest and utility to computer hardware specialists, programmers, systems analysts, operations researchers, and mathematicians. •

Volume 1: *Abacus to Arithmetic*

CONTENTS

Abacus, *J. Belzer.* Abstract Algebra, *M. Perlman.* Abstracting, *B. Mathis and J. Rush.* Abstracting Services, *M. Weinstock.* Acceleration Methods, *J. Wimp.* Access and Accessing, *P. Meissner and F. Martin.* Accounting for Computer Usage, *E. Miles, Jr.* Ac-

(continued)

counting, Computers in, *D. Li.* Accumulator, *T. Trygar.* Accuracy, *G. Moshos.* Acoustic Memories, *C. Smith.* Adaptive and Learning Systems, *W. Jacobs.* Address—Addressing, *J. Belzer.* Administrative Systems and Data Processing, *D. Teichroew.* Advanced Planning, Computers in, *H. Linstone.* The ARPA Network, *H. Frank.* The Aerospace Corporation Digital Computing Capability, *R. Van Vranken.* Airline Reservation Systems, *T. Wendel.* Alexander, Samuel, *M. Fox.* Algeria, Data Processing in, *Y. Mentalecheta.* ALGOL, *J. Belzer.* Algorithm, *A. Anderson.* Allocation Models, *S. Elmaghraby and M. El-Kammash.* Alphabets, *M. Grems.* Alpha systems, *A. Ershov.* American Chemical Society—Chemical Abstracts Service, *G. Gautney, Jr. and R. Wigington.* American Federation of Information Processing, *B. Gilchrist and R. Tanaka.* American Institute of Certified Public Accountants, *N. Zakin.* American Institute of Civil Engineers with Emphasis on the Use of Computers, *J. Cobb, Jr.* American Institute of Industrial Engineers, Computers in, *J. Bailey and V. Sahney.* American Institute of Physics, *R. Lerner.* American Management Association, *J. Enell and J. Alexander.* American Mathematical Society, *G. Walker.* American Records Management Association, *R. Grimes.* American Society of Civil Engineers, Computers in, *J. Fleming.* American Society for Information Science, *R. McAfee.* American Statistical Association, Computers and Statistics, *A. Goodman.* Amplifiers, Operational *K. Oka.* The AN/FSQ-7, *E. Wenzel.* Analog Signals and Analog Data Processing, *W. Karplus.* Analog-Digital Conversion, *B. Stephenson.* Analysis of Variance, *H. Ginsburg.* "AND" or "NOT", "NAND" and "NOR" logic, *M. Mickle.* Annual Review of Information Science and Technology, *C. Cuadra.* APL Terminal System, *H. Katzan, Jr.* Approximation Methods, *G. Byrne.* APT (Automatically Programmed Tools), *J. Goodrich and R. Thrush.* Argentina, Computers in, *M. Milchberg.* Argonne National Laboratory Computer Center, *M. Butler.* Arithmetic Operations, *C. Donaghey.*

ENCYCLOPEDIA OF LIBRARY AND INFORMATION SCIENCE

in multi-volumes

editors: ALLEN KENT and HAROLD LANCOUR

assistant editor: WILLIAM Z. NASRI
Graduate School of Library and Information Sciences and The Knowledge Availability Systems Center, University of Pittsburgh

Subscription price: $40 per volume
Single volume price: $50 per volume

ADVISORY BOARD

Olga S. Akhamova, *U.S.S.R.* • Jack Belzer, *U.S.A.* • Charles P. Bourne, *U.S.A.* • Douglas Bryant, *U.S.A.* • David H. Clift, *U.S.A.* • Jay E. Daily, *U.S.A.* • Robert B. Downs, *U.S.A.* • Sir Frank Francis, *England* • Emerson Greenaway, *U.S.A.* • Cloyd Dake Gull, *U.S.A.* • Shigenori Hamada, *Japan* • J. Clement Harrison, *U.S.A.* • Donald J. Hillman, *U.S.A.* • J. Phillips Immroth, *U.S.A.* • William V. Jackson, *U.S.A.* • B. S. Kesavan, *India* • Preben Kirkegaard, *Denmark* • W. Kenneth Lowry, *U.S.A.* • Kalu Okorie, *Nigeria* • E. Pietsch, *Germany* • S. R. Ranganathan, *India* • Samuel Rothstein, *Canada* • Nasser Sharify, *U.S.A.* • Marietta Daniels Shepard, *U.S.A.* • Vladimir Slamecka, *U.S.A.* • Mary Elizabeth Stevens, *U.S.A.* • Roy B. Stokes, *England* • C. Walter Stone, *U.S.A.* • Josef Stummvoll, *Austria* • Orrin E. Taulbee, *U.S.A.* • Lawrence S. Thompson, *U.S.A.* • Eileen Thornton, *U.S.A.* • L. J. van der Wolk, *Holland* • B. C. Vickery, *England* • Bill M. Woods, *U.S.A.*

Up to this time there has not been available a single source containing a comprehensive and unified treatment of the fields of both library science and information science. This multi-volume *Encyclopedia* is the first complete and authoritative work on library science and information science, combining both theory and practice of the two fields in the United States and abroad. The *Encyclopedia* provides a source of easy access, ready reference, and comprehensive coverage of the concepts, terms, methods, and important personages of the two fields, and displays and enhances the essential interdependence of the two areas.

Volume 9: Fore-Edge to Grabhorn   700 pages, illustrated. 1973

CONTENTS

Fore-Edge Painting, *A. Skoog* • Forest Press, Inc., *R. Sealock* • Forgeries, Frauds, Etc., *L. Thompson* • Format, Catalog, *J. Daily* • FORTRAN, *J. Williams* • France, Libraries in,

P. Salvan • France, Library and Information Science, Current Issues in, *E. de Grolier* • Frankfurt Book Fair, *S. Taubert* • Franklin, Benjamin, *W. Nasri* • Franklin Book Programs, *J. Daily* • Franklin D. Roosevelt Library, *J. Marshall* • Franklin Institute Library, *E. Hilker* • Free Libraries, *S. Jackson* • Free Library of Philadelphia, *K. Doms* • Friends of Libraries, *S. Wallace* • Fugitive Materials, *N. Bowman* • Funding—Library Endowments in the United States, *W. Jackson* • G.E. 250 Information Searching Selector, *A. Kent* • Game Theory, *A. Holzman* • Garamond, Claude, *J. Dearden* • Genealogical Libraries and Collections, *G. Doane* • General Semantics, *C. Read* • Gennadi, Grigorily Nikolaevich, *O. Akhmanova* • Geographical Codes, *K. Kansky* • Geographical Libraries and Map Collections, *J. Wolter* • Geographical Literature, *N. Corley* • Geological Libraries and Collections, *G. Lea, P. Briers, and A. Harvey* • Geological Literature, *G. Lea, J. Diment, and A. Harvey* • George Peabody College, School of Library Science, *E. Gleaves* • (The George Washington University, the Medical Center), Biological Sciences Communication Project, *R. Wise* • Georgia Institute of Technology, School of Information and Computer Science, *V. Slamecka* • Georgia Library Association, *D. Estes* • German Union Catalog, *R. Stueart* • Germany, Libraries and Information Centers in, *E. Pietsch, H. Fuchs, H. Ernestus, D. Oertel, M. Cremer, H. Arntz, C. Muller, K. Buschbeck, and K. Schubarth-Engelschall* • Ghana, Libraries in, *E. Amedekey* • Gifts and Exchanges, *J. DePew* • Glasgow, University of Glasgow Library, *R. MacKenna* • Golden Cockerel Press, The, *R. Cave* • Gorbunov-Posadov Ivan Ivanovich, *O. Akhmanova* • Government Publications (Documents), *J. Childs* • Government Printing Office, *C. Buckley* • Grabhorn Press, *R. Bell*

More detailed information on our encyclopedias is available upon request.